CHAPTER 1

The Basics of Burgers

We're big burger fans, as we're sure you are. Before we started cooking whole hogs on 5,000-pound mobile barbecue pits, before we started winning the biggest, baddest barbecue contests in the world, we cooked burgers—lots of burgers. First for ourselves, then for just about everybody we knew. And we got pretty good at it.

We still love to cook burgers, whether it's for a crowd, at the restaurants, or just for the family. In this book, we give you the information and skills you'll need to make what we believe is the perfect burger at home. We got there by dissecting the steps necessary to making a simple, juicy, delicious patty with a nicely seared crust. The kind that will make your friends stop in their tracks and ask, "How did you do that?" It's not terribly complicated, but it takes some time and attention. We also provide options to dress the burgers up a bit—or sometimes, more than a bit. Because, while we love the perfect simplicity of a well-prepared burger, we also love ramping it up and taking it a few steps beyond.

So what you will find in these pages are techniques for grinding and shaping meat, poultry, and fish into patties; our favorite cooking techniques; and recipes for amazing burgers, killer toppings, side dishes, and delicious, frothy beverages. We even have a dessert burger.

Burger Lore

There have been many claims by those who say they invented the hamburger in the United States around the turn of the twentieth century. Some of the stories are pretty impressive. But none of them can be proved beyond a doubt. It's widely agreed that initially, the hamburger emigrated from Hamburg, Germany, in the form of chopped, minced, or scraped beef. Once it arrived, it was renamed "Hamburg steak."

The evolution from minced meat served on a plate with silverware to the handheld patty on a bun most of us grew up craving is a little harder to track. Among the claims of the first burger is one from Charlie Nagreen, who said he sold meatballs sandwiched between two slices of bread from an ox-drawn cart at a county fair in Wisconsin in 1885. That same year, Frank and Charles Menches of Ohio reportedly sold ground beef sandwiches at the Erie County Fair in Hamburg, New York.

Louis' Lunch, in New Haven, Connecticut, claims to be the birthplace of the "hamburger sandwich." Open by Louis Lassen in 1895 and run by his family since, Louis' cooks its patties in the same cast-iron vertical broilers that have been on-site for more than 100 years. But these patties come on toasted white bread, not buns, causing some to question whether they can, in fact, be considered true burgers.

Some say the Bilby family invented the hamburger on a bun at a family picnic outside Tulsa, Oklahoma, on July 4, 1891—more than forty years before they even opened their drive-in restaurant, Weber's Superior Root Beer Drive-In. Patriarch Oscar Bilby also created the cast-iron grill he used to cook the all-beef patties; his wife, Fanny, made the sourdough buns. Weber's is still owned by family members, and burgers are still cooked in Oscar's original grill (and served with his root beer).

But then there's fry cook Walter Anderson, who opened a hamburger stand in Wichita, Kansas, in 1916. He is credited with being the first to cook burgers on a very hot grill, flatten them with a spatula while cooking, and probably most important, serving them on special buns. (More special than Fanny Bilby's? We'll never know.) He expanded his little business to three stands, at which point his real estate agent, Billy Ingram, became his business partner. The result of their partnership is White Castle, the first fast-food hamburger chain.

There has been continuous evolution since the early 1920s. Today, under the burger umbrella we eat a dizzying array of patties on a wide range of buns. For most of us, whether it's made of beef, pork, chicken, seafood, vegetables, grains, or some combination, a burger is the ultimate comfort food. Dress it up. Keep it simple. It doesn't matter. It's usually what you're in the mood for. Add some fries and a thick, cold drink, and it satisfies just about any craving.

Contents

Foreword	6
CHAPTER 1: THE BASICS OF BURGERS	9
CHAPTER 2: BURGERS 101	19
CHAPTER 3: NEW AMERICAN CLASSICS	49
CHAPTER 4: WHERE'S THE BEEF?	79
CHAPTER 5: BURGERS BEYOND BORDERS	97
CHAPTER 6: YOU WANT FRIES WITH THAT?	115
CHAPTER 7: THAT'S A FRAPPE!	125
Resources	138
About the Authors	140
Index	141

Foreword
Originally appeared in *Wicked Good Burgers* (Fair Winds Press 2013)

When I first heard that Andy Husbands and Chris Hart, the diabolically clever minds behind the championship barbecue team IQUE, were at work on a hamburger book, my first emotion was a queasy dread. But then I brightened up. Husbands and Hart are the most innovative cooks in the barbecue world; their ability to transcend the cast-iron prison of conventional smoke cooking represents the most liberating thing to happen to barbecue since the invention of coal. But, while the techniques and technology of cooking it have changed (for the worse), the basic flavors and recipes are the same (or worse.) That was what was so amazing about IQUE: As a paradox, this can hardly be overstated. It's as if North Korea were to finance Christo's latest project or a Civil War re-enactment society producing a white paper outlining a post-national paradigm for counter-insurgency operations. Unless you've had to judge it, you can't believe how stultified and conventional the world of competition barbecue is; and it would be equally hard to express how singularly elegant IQUE's work is, by any standard.

But where barbecue is in desperate need of innovation, the burger is besieged by it—at least, from the point of view of an arch-conservative, such as myself. "The orthodox cheeseburger," I once rhapsodized in *Time*, "with its pillowy, enriched white bun, Pythagorean square of tangerine-colored American cheese and blissfully unadulterated (and unspiced) beef is an invention that cannot really be improved upon. Like sashimi or peaches and cream, it's a gastronomic end point." My skepticism was primed by a long entrenched dogmatism. Did we really need a book of grotesque toppings, freakish cheeses, and unnatural protein swaps? My idea of a perfect hamburger cookbook would be one page long. But then I read *Wicked Good Burgers*.

Johnson famously defined wonder as "the effect of novelty upon ignorance." I tried out several of these burgers, expecting to despise them. A tortilla-wrapped chile burger? Really? How could that not be bad? And yet I found the same clarity and force in their burger innovations as I had in their barbecue ones. I was also reassured in seeing that this book wasn't just a compendium of zany recipes, as these hamburger books so frequently are. Those books, in trying to deface our great national dish, evince all the desperation of a divorced dad hitting the singles bars in a newly bought hip outfit. But *Wicked Good Burgers* begins with a rock-solid fundament: how to mix and blend burger meat—which is far and away the most important element of burger cookery and without which no hamburger book should be taken seriously.

But beyond that, anybody who has ever eaten at Andy's restaurant, Tremont 647, or IQUE's barbecue, knows that these guys have a deep mastery of meat; they don't lay on flavors randomly. Every one of the burgers in this book—including my own humble contribution—is deeply felt and much-practiced. I may disagree with some of Andy and Chris's predilections, such as fancy (brioche?!) buns and cheddar cheese, both of which I find grossly out of place in any self-respecting burger or cheeseburger, but in their hands it somehow comes out right. Again and again, in trying these recipes, I have found the limits of my own bigotry and the widening expanse of my admiration for these guys. So, yes, I was wrong and they were right. I hope to eat a hamburger with them soon to tell them as much.

—Josh Ozersky New York City, 2012

Why Grind Your Meat

The most important factor for great burgers—whether you're talking basic hamburger or some other configuration—is outstanding ingredients. As long as you get your meat, fish, or poultry from a purveyor you trust, you're off to a great start. But we're control freaks, and as good as freshly ground beef is from the butcher, it's that much better when we do it ourselves. It takes a bit more work, but the payoff is well worth it, for a number of reasons.

First, the fresher the meat is the better your burger will be, and there is nothing fresher than just-ground. It's kind of like coffee. You can buy preground beans, but even if you buy the highest quality, most beautifully roasted beans available, unless you grind them right before brewing, your cup will not be as transcendent as it could be. (So if you don't grind your own beans, you should seriously consider it.) Freshness matters.

Grinding your meat/poultry/fish also gives you a lot more control over the final product. Most butchers use all chuck for ground beef, which makes delicious hamburgers. But when you grind your own you can combine cuts, like brisket, short rib, and chuck (our favorite mix). You can control the meat-to-fat ratio. And you can mix in spices and other flavorings, like salt, which helps the proteins bind together, and our Fifth Dimension Powder (page 25). The result will be burgers of superior flavor and juiciness.

Special Burger Blends

We call for chuck as our standard burger meat because it has the perfect meat-to-fat ratio—80 percent meat to 20 percent fat, or 80/20. When we want to enhance the flavor and texture, we grind it with other cuts of beef. Following are guidelines for making your own blends, based on the 1½-pound (680 g) portions we use in the majority of the recipes in this book. But don't feel constrained by what we list here. Feel free to experiment and come up with your own combinations. That's the beauty of grinding your own meat.

1 pound (455 g) freshly ground chuck

½ pound (225 g) total weight of one or more of the following:

- Short ribs—This gives burgers extra fat and intense beefy flavor; it's a good choice if you will be cooking the burgers beyond medium-rare.

- Brisket—This adds tangy, earthy flavor. Use the point for more fat, which makes the burgers juicier.

- Dry-aged strip steak—This special cut adds a musky, concentrated beef flavor.

- Beef cheeks—These are lean and tough, but if they are cooked for a long time they become incredibly tender. When ground with chuck for burgers, they make the blend rich and unctuous.

- Skirt steak—This adds meaty texture and is a beef lover's favorite.

The Basics of Burgers 11

Slice excess fat from top of beef chuck.

Cut large piece in half.

Begin slicing chuck.

Chuck is ready for his close-up.

Slices should be same width as mouth of grinder.

Chuck slices ready for grinding

Quick and Easy Burger Cookbook

You can also add ¼ pound (115 g) of one of the following. If you opt to do this, reduce the chuck by ¾ pound (115 g).

- Beef Marrow—This gives burgers a rich, intense umami bomb. Your guests will be agog at your burger prowess.

- Pork fat—Do you like your burgers juicy? Get ready for a gusher.

- Bacon—For smoky, peppery burgers, add a few strips of sliced, uncooked bacon.

How to Grind Your Meat

To get started grinding at home, at minimum you will need a stand mixer with a grinder attachment. These usually come with two grinding plates—coarse and fine. Most of our burger recipes call for the meat to be ground with the coarse plate. The fine plate is more appropriate for sausages, forcemeat, and some charcuterie. Another option is a standalone meat grinder (see Resources, page 138).

The grinder's many moving parts create friction, which in turn creates heat, something you want to avoid for a couple of reasons. First, it increases the possibility of bacteria growth, a potential health risk. Second, heat will melt the fat slowly. If the fat melts, the meat and fat won't emulsify, and you will be left with dry, crumbly burgers. One of the solutions is to freeze all the grinder parts. We just store ours in the freezer. So whenever we're overcome by the urge to grind some meat—not as gruesome as it might sound—we're ready to go.

We also freeze the meat before we grind it. It is much easier to work with this way and you won't

have to worry as much about the fat melting. You want the meat to be stiff, but not completely frozen. Cut the meat into long strips that are the width of the grinder opening and put it in the freezer for 30 to 60 minutes. Then process the meat using the coarse grinder plate (medium, if you're using a standalone meat grinder). Follow the shaping instructions below or, if you're not going to use the meat immediately, shape it into a loaf form, cover it with plastic wrap, and refrigerate it for up to two days.

Shaping Your Burgers

We try to handle the meat as little as possible and keep it as cold as possible. It's a good idea to wash your hands with very cold water, to lower their temperature, before you start to shape the burgers. But be sure to dry them very carefully; even though you don't want your burgers to become dry, you certainly don't want 'em wet.

Most of the recipes in this book are for 6-ounce (170 g) burgers. We highly recommend weighing the meat before you begin shaping. A kitchen scale is an incredibly useful tool to have around. If you don't have one, there are several options that won't break the bank (see Resources, page 138).

After grinding (or if you're starting with already ground meat), separate the meat into 6-ounce (170 g) portions and roll them into loose balls. Pat and shape them into rounds that are about ½-inch (1 cm) thick. Don't pack them too tight. Using two fingers, make a dimple in the center of each burger, about ¾-inch (6 mm) deep and an inch (2.5 cm) wide. This will ensure that the burger does not puff up like a meatball while cooking.

Burgers on a skillet—Chris's favorite cooking method

Andy's preference—cooking over live fire

Cooking Methods

Not that we're closed-minded or anything, but as far as we're concerned, there are two primary ways to cook burgers—on a griddle/skillet or over a wood-fired and charcoal grill. We like these methods because the high heat they yield creates a superior Maillard reaction, resulting in a crunchy, caramelized sear. We can be flexible enough to accept that not everybody sees it our way, but we stand firm in our conviction that these two methods will produce the tastiest, juiciest burgers.

So settle in. Here's our brief tutorial. And you thought burgers were simple . . .

Griddle/Skillet (Chris's Favorite)

When you cook burgers on a griddle or skillet, it's important that the surface of the pan be hot. We recommend about 500°F (250°C)—or smoking hot when you brush it with oil. Most often you will likely do this on your kitchen stove, but we love to use our skillet directly over a charcoal grill (gas works, too). It's easy to get it hot and avoids the mess of oil splattering indoors. This will give you a beautiful char on the outside of the burger while allowing it to stay juicy and tender inside.

In general, we recommend the following:

Brush a very hot griddle with vegetable oil (a silicone brush works well for this, if you don't want to destroy all of your brushes).

One of the main benefits of a griddle is developing a crust across the entire surface of the burger, so always use a flat-surfaced, not ridged, griddle.

Place burger patties on the griddle, without overcrowding them.

Cook 2 to 3 minutes per side, depending on the thickness of the burgers and desired doneness. Never press down on the burger while it's cooking (okay when raw). Once the fat has heated up, pressing down on the burger will just push out the juices, which you don't want to do.

Transfer the burgers to a platter; if you would like cheese, add it now. Tent burgers with foil and allow them to rest for 3 to 5 minutes.

Serve.

Wood-Fired and Charcoal Grilling (Andy's Favorite)

What tastes better than burgers cooked over live fire, with that charcoal flavor infused into the meat, fish, or poultry sizzling on the grate? It's what summer is all about, at least for us in New England and for those of you lucky enough to have outdoor cooking weather year-round.

Live-fire cooking is not as predictable as the stovetop method and requires some practice.

Here's how to get the best results from your fire:

Line the bottom of a kettle grill with charcoal: not too much, just enough to cover.

Fill a charcoal chimney with hardwood lump charcoal, crumple two pieces of newspaper and stuff them below the coals, and light the newspaper. Wait about 10 minutes for the charcoal to become fully ignited. Flames should be just starting to peek through the top of the pile.

Carefully, wearing heatproof gloves, pour the lit charcoal evenly over the bed of unlit charcoal.

When the fire is medium-hot or very hot (depending on the recipe), sprinkle wood chips over the fire. Don't soak the chips; plenty of smoke will be created. (For a medium-hot fire, you should be able to hold your hands over the coals for 10 seconds; for very hot, you should be able to hold your hands over for 5 seconds.)

Place the burgers on the grill grate and cook for 2 to 3 minutes per side, depending on the thickness of the burgers and desired doneness.

Transfer the burgers to a platter; if you would like cheese, add it now. Tent burgers with foil and allow them to rest for 3 to 5 minutes.

Serve.

WHY DOES MY BURGER NEED TO REST?

Most of the recipes in this book call for resting time for the burgers—And for good reason. If you cut into the burger immediately, the juices will end up on the plate, instead of in your mouth. Resting allows the juices to redistribute throughout the burger. Also, during this period, the meat continues to cook. Our internal temperature guidelines take that into consideration.

The Basics of Burgers 15

Some of our recipes call for grilling over a two-zone fire. To do this, instead of spreading the coals over the bottom of the grill, pour the charcoal so it piles up against one side of the kettle. Then, when you are ready to add the charcoal from the chimney, just pour it over the unlit charcoal. One side of the grill will have an active fire going, and the other side will have no charcoal at all.

Equipment

There are a few pieces of equipment that we feel are essential to making perfect burgers; and there are others that we highly recommend. Our Resources section (see page 138) will help you find all these items and more.

Griddles/Skillets

When cooking on a skillet or griddle, one of the most important features to look for is the ability to maintain consistent heat level. Yes, you want the surface to be very hot, but you also want the temperature to remain hot consistently. We recommend using pans that are made of a heavy, thick metal that will retain the heat and not drop in temperature when you add the burgers.

Cast iron—We prefer cast-iron skillets because it is the best material for maintaining heat. Cast-iron skillets last forever and season beautifully, developing a natural nonstick surface as they age. They are also reasonably priced. You have to clean the skillets well after every use (check the manufacturer's usage guide) because cast iron is porous and can retain the flavor of whatever you last cooked. You don't want your beef burger to taste like last night's salmon burger—delicious as it may have been.

Stainless steel is another excellent option. Stainless steel griddles and pans are coated over cast iron, so they have that material's heat retention property without the porousness. If you maintain them well, they are nearly nonstick.

Always avoid pans and skillets that have a nonstick surface applied. When you get to temperatures of 500°F (250°C), there is the potential for the nonstick material to burn, break off, and end up in your food—Not very tasty.

Grinders

Grinder attachments—Attachments, available for most stand mixers, are perfect for grinding small amounts of meat. If you have a stand mixer, this is the easiest way for you to take your first steps toward home grinding.

Standalone meat grinders—These are also available for home cooks. We like the Weston #10, a classic, old-school, hand-crank model. This inexpensive, table-mounted grinder is great for small amounts of grinding. The STX Turbo Force 3000 is more than a great name (doesn't it sound like a Chuck Norris movie?). It's a perfect midlevel grinder for the home. For serious home chefs who want to show who makes the best burgers for the greatest number of people, LEM Products' electric grinders are the Cadillacs of home machines. We like the sound of the Big Bite. We still recommend keeping the parts in the freezer, just to be extra cautious.

Grills

Kettle grills—These are probably the most common piece of charcoal-fired outdoor cooking equipment. You can cook almost all the recipes in this book with a 22-inch (55 cm) kettle grill. We are big Weber fans. They are reasonably priced, very portable, work beautifully, and last for years.

Gas—We don't use gas grills, but we understand that some people appreciate their convenience. Our friend Steve Sheinkopf, who owns one of New England's largest appliance stores, lists two Weber gas grills among his top four. The higher-end Weber Summit is a high-power grill with rotisserie, smoker, and sear features, for under $2,500. The much more affordable Weber Spirit is "fine for most," he says, at around $400. Its price is similar to other manufacturers, but it should last a lot longer.

Thermometers

Infrared—This is a must for skillet cooking. Simply point it at your skillet and you will know right away whether the cooking surface is hot enough to start cooking.

Instant-read thermometer—There are a couple of different styles. We like the pocket-sized Thermapen thermometer that tells the temperature of your food instantly.

Probe thermometer—These nifty little devices let you monitor the air temperature in your smoker and the food temperature without having to open the cooker.

Everything Else

Deep fryers—A deep fryer isn't essential for perfectly crisp french fries and onion rings, but it makes the job a lot easier and less messy. The most important feature to look for is recovery time; basically, how long does it take to get back up to its original set temperature? The faster this happens, the less grease will be absorbed into the

food being fried. The Breville Deep Fryer is our favorite home machine. It heats quickly and stays hot. The DeLonghi Dual Zone Fryer has a large capacity and is a good midlevel fryer. And Presto's Fry Daddy is inexpensive and fine for small amounts of cooking.

Sous vide cooker—It is possible to create your own sous vide–style cooking environment (cooking vacuum-sealed food in a water bath at low temperature for a longer time than in a conventional oven) using a slow cooker. These homemade rigs are not super accurate but work well for some dishes. When you cook burgers sous vide, though, it's important to maintain a very accurate low temperature—we recommend $120°$ to $125°F$ (49 to $52°C$). If you are just a few degrees off, the medium-rare burger you were aiming for will turn out medium. For this reason, we highly recommend a Sous Vide Supreme water oven. It is the best way to accurately control the temperatures and successfully replicate the cooking method that is making its way increasingly from professional to home kitchens.

Drink mixer—Most home blenders do an adequate job of mixing milk, syrup, and ice cream into a thick, frothy drink, but the smaller blade on soda fountain–style drink mixers uses a different motion than the blender's knife-like blades, resulting in a thicker drink with a more even texture. We use the Hamilton Beach DrinkMaster Drink Mixer to get malt shop–quality drinks.

CHAPTER 2

Burgers 101

Making a good burger is easy. But making what we believe is a perfect burger takes a little more effort. To us, perfection is the whole package—the meat, the condiments, and the bun. We've had really delicious burgers that are ruined because they're served on soggy buns; the pickles taste terrible; or the ketchup is old and crusty and there's no mayo—one of our favorite toppings. Conversely, we've had burgers served on beautiful, fresh buns with the best mustard, sautéed mushrooms, and caramelized onions we've ever tasted and flawlessly crispy, salty french fries; but the meat is cooked until it's gray and tasteless. What a waste of ingredients!

In this chapter, we obsessed over all the details, so you don't have to. The result is what we believe is the best technique for grinding, shaping, and cooking Our Perfect Burger and Our Perfect Turkey Burger. We also offer a comprehensive selection of Wicked Killer Burger Toppings that range from Tomato-Ginger Ketchup to Pig Candy (as addictive as it sounds). And we include a couple of bun recipes that are delicious complements to any burger in the book.

Perfection's not so hard.

Our Perfect Burger

We can't stress enough how important the quality of the meat, the grind, the shaping, and cooking technique are to a burger. If even one of the elements is off, you can have a good burger, even a really good one, but it won't be perfect. Condiments and rolls do a lot to enhance burgers, but a truly great burger should be able to stand on its own—Delicious naked, if you will. That is the kind of burger we've created here. Though we're not suggesting you eat it naked.

If you want to give your burgers an extra flavor boost, be sure to add the Fifth Dimension Powder. Or you can use ½ teaspoon (2.5 g) kosher salt.

1½ pounds (680 g) beef chuck or ground chuck from your favorite butcher, or your favorite combination (See "Special Burger Blends," pages 11–13.)

1½ tablespoons (11 g) Fifth Dimension Powder (page 25) or ½ teaspoon (2.5 g) kosher salt

Vegetable oil, for cooking

Kosher salt and fresh cracked black pepper, to taste

4 slices deli-style American cheese, optional

4 Flour Bakery Burger Buns (page 46) or Katie's Burger Buns (page 45)

—
Yield: 4 burgers

Freeze the chuck until frozen but not stiff, about 1 hour. Remove from the freezer and season with Fifth Dimension Powder or ½ teaspoon (2.5 g) kosher salt. Grind the chuck according to the technique in chapter 1 (page 13). If you're using ground chuck, mix in the Fifth Dimension Powder or ½ teaspoon (2.5 g) kosher salt. Refrigerate while you prepare the skillet.

Heat the skillet over high heat until very hot. If you have an infrared thermometer, the skillet should register at least 500°F (250°C). Or test by brushing on a bit of oil. When the skillet starts to smoke, it is ready.

Remove the chuck from the refrigerator. Divide into four 6-ounce (170 g) portions and shape the patties according to technique in chapter 1 (page 13). Season with salt and pepper.

Brush the skillet with oil and arrange the patties without overcrowding. Cook for 3 minutes. Turn the patties over and cook for 2 minutes more. If you like your burgers rare (which we recommend), the internal temperature should register 120° to 125°F (49° to 52°C); medium-rare burgers should have an internal temperature of 130° to 135°F (54° to 57°C). We don't want to know about it if you cook your burgers any more than that. (See sidebar on page 22.)

Transfer the burgers to a platter and lay a slice of cheese on top if desired. Tent the platter with foil and allow the burgers to rest for 3 to 5 minutes.

continued

Our Perfect Burger *(continued)*

Alternatively, you can grill the burgers. Prepare the grill and follow the instructions in the Wood-Fired and Charcoal Grilling section in chapter 1 (pages 15–16).

To serve: Place the burgers on the bottom halves of the buns. Spread Best.Mayo.Ever. (recipe follows) and/or mustard on the top halves and add your favorite toppings. Our preferences are cold, crispy iceberg lettuce, thinly sliced tomatoes (in-season only), Caramelized Onions (page 26), Gram's Bread-and-Butter Pickles (page 107), and any of the Wicked Killer Burger Toppings in this chapter.

DONENESS TEMPERATURES

We like our burgers on the rare side—pink, juicy, practically bleeding. but The USDA recommends, for safety's sake, cooking all ground meat to 160°F (71°C). We believe if you know where your meat comes from and grind it yourself—or have it ground by a trusted butcher—you are going to be fine. But you have to do what feels, and tastes, right to you. young children, elderly people, and those with compromised immune systems should play it safe and eat their burgers well done. For everyone else, here are temperature guidelines

Rare: 120°–125°F (49°–52°C)

Medium Rare: 130°–135°F (54°–57°C)

Medium: 140°–145°F (60°–63°C)

Medium Well: 150°–155°F (66°–68°C)

Well Done: 160°F (71°C) and higher

Best.Mayo.Ever.

Hands down, this is one of our favorite items to spread on a burger or to dip our fries in. Technically, the addition of garlic powder makes it an aioli because the simplest definition of aioli is a garlic mayonnaise. But we don't want to get hung up on semantics. We think this is the best mayo ever. And when you see how easy it is to make, you may never purchase the jarred stuff again.

2 egg yolks

1 teaspoon (5 g) Dijon mustard

3 tablespoons (45 ml)
white vinegar

½ teaspoon (2.5 ml)
Worcestershire sauce

3 cups (700 ml) canola
or vegetable oil

½ teaspoon (2.5 g) kosher salt

1 teaspoon (5 g) large,
thin-flaked sea salt, such
as Maldon sea salt

1 teaspoon (3 g) garlic powder

—
Yield: 3½ cups (800 g)

In the bowl of a stand mixer with the whisk attachment, mix the egg yolks, mustard, vinegar, and Worcestershire sauce on medium-high speed for 2 minutes until light and fully incorporated.

Very slowly stream in the oil to make the emulsion. You will see the mixture will start to thicken and become increasingly pale. Continue pouring the oil in slowly until it is thick like mayonnaise in a jar, about 4 minutes. Turn the mixer off and add the two salts and garlic powder. Mix on medium high for 1 minute more.

Remove from the bowl and refrigerate until needed, up to 1 week.

Fifth Dimension Powder

Recently, there has been a lot of talk about the umami factor, or the fifth taste. Umami gives foods a savory, over-the-top flavor that makes you want to have another bite, and another, and another.

We created this mixture to take our burgers over the top. Ideally, you should add it when you are grinding your meat since it becomes fully incorporated that way. We add a little over 1 tablespoon (14 g) per pound of meat. If you are folding it in by hand, make sure to mix it well.

The goal of this blend is to flavor the meat but not make its presence known; rather, to entice everyone to have another bite and wonder, 'what makes this so good?'

6 tablespoons (45 g) porcini powder (see Resources, page 138)

2 tablespoons (15 g) portobello powder (see Resources, page 138)

2 tablespoons (15 g) Worcestershire powder (see Resources, page 138)

2 tablespoons (14 g) onion powder

2 tablespoons (18 g) garlic powder

—

Yield: About 1 cup (227 g) enough for 14 to 16 burgers

In a small bowl, mix all ingredients together. Store in an airtight container in a cool, dark place for up to 6 months.

Burgers 101 25

Gram's Bread and Butter Pickles

Chris's wife, Jenny, grew up on these pickles that her mother, Mary, made. They are a perfect accompaniment to burgers, any casual meal, or snacking on by themselves. This is an easy starter recipe for anybody intimidated by canning and pickling.

4 quarts (4 L) pickling cucumbers, sliced into ⅛-inch (3 mm) thick coins

8 small yellow onions, thinly sliced

1 green pepper, cored and seeded, thinly sliced

1 red pepper, cored and seeded, thinly sliced

3 cloves garlic, sliced

⅓ cup (96 g) pickling and canning salt

4 cups ice cubes, to cover (or more if necessary)

BRINE
3 cups (600 g) sugar

3 cups (700 ml) cider vinegar

2 tablespoons (22 g) mustard seed

2 teaspoons (4.4 g) turmeric

2 teaspoons (4 g) celery seed

1 teaspoon (2 g) ground black pepper

—

Yield: 3½ quarts (3.5 L)

Combine the cucumbers, onions, peppers, and garlic in a large bowl. Sprinkle salt over top, and then mix with your hands to distribute thoroughly. Cover with ice cubes. Let stand 2 to 3 hours; drain and rinse well, making sure to remove all salt.

In a large pot over medium-high heat, bring the brine ingredients to a boil, stirring to dissolve the sugar. Add the vegetables and bring to boil. Remove the pot from the heat.

While the vegetables are boiling, sterilize three 1-quart (1 L) and one 1-pint (475 ml) mason jars and lids. Wash the jars, lids, and screw bands in hot, soapy water and rinse well. Dry the screw bands and set aside. Heat the jars in simmering water (200°F [93°C]) in a deep 8- to 10-quart (8 to 10 L) pot and place the lids in a saucepan of simmering water until ready to use.

When the vegetables are ready, remove the jars and lids from the pots. Ladle the hot vegetables and brine into the jars, leaving ¾-inch (6 mm) space at the top. Wipe the sides of the jars, tightly seal, and return to the pot, making sure there is enough water to cover the jars by 1 to 2 inches (2.5 to 5 cm). Cover the pot and bring the water to a boil. Process for 10 minutes. Turn off the heat, remove the cover, and allow the jars to sit in the water for 5 minutes. Remove the jars from the water and leave at room temperature for 12 to 24 hours.

Store at room temperature for up to 6 months. Refrigerate after opening.

Our Perfect Turkey Burger

One of the biggest complaints about turkey burgers is that they can be dry. We take a two-pronged approach to that problem. First, we use only dark meat, which has more fat and flavor than breast meat. Second, we add a few ingredients to keep things moist. The fact that they make the burgers wildly flavorful is an added bonus. We recommend grilling these burgers because we love the flavor that fire adds. But if you want to cook them indoors, starting on the stovetop and finishing in the oven ensures that they stay juicy, with a nice crust. In our experience, even people who think they hate turkey burgers love these.

1 head garlic

2½ pounds (1.1 kg) ground dark-meat turkey

1 tablespoon (15 ml) Worcestershire sauce

2 teaspoons (10 ml) soy sauce

¾ cup (15 g) chopped fresh parsley

1 egg, beaten

½ cup (60 g) fine dry bread crumbs

Vegetable oil, for cooking

6 Katie's Burger Buns (page 45) or whole wheat sesame buns

RECOMMENDED CONDIMENTS: romaine lettuce, Kewpie mayonnaise, Sriracha, Quick-Pickled Onions (page 57), chopped scallions, Glo's Bean Salad (recipe follows)

—

Yield: 6 burgers

Preheat oven to 325°F (170°C, gas mark 3). Wrap the garlic in tin foil and roast for 1 hour. Squeeze out the cloves and mash with a fork.

In a large bowl, mix the ground turkey with the mashed garlic, Worcestershire and soy sauces, and parsley. Fold in the egg and half of the bread crumbs. Gradually add the remaining bread crumbs until the turkey mixture is no longer sticky. You may not have to add the full ½ cup (60 g).

Divide the mixture into 6 even portions and shape into patties according to the technique in chapter 1 (page 13). Refrigerate until ready to cook.

If grilling, prepare the grill according to the instructions for Wood Fire and Charcoal Grilling in chapter 1 (pages 15–16). Clean the grill grate well with a stiff wire brush.

When the fire is ready, remove the burgers from the refrigerator. Brush the oil on the grill grate. Set the burgers on the grate directly over coals and grill for 5 minutes per side.

If you're cooking indoors, preheat the oven to 325°F (170°C, gas mark 3).

Heat a heavy, cast-iron skillet over high heat until very hot. If you have an infrared thermometer, the skillet should register at least 500°F (250°C). You can also test by brushing a bit of oil on the skillet.

When the skillet starts to smoke, it is ready. Brush the griddle with vegetable oil to cover completely.

continued

Our Perfect Turkey Burger *(continued)*

Place the patties in the skillet without overcrowding. Cook for 3 minutes. Turn the patties over and cook for 2 minutes on the other side. Transfer the patties to a baking sheet and bake for 7 to 8 minutes or until their internal temperature registers 160°F (71°C). Remove from the oven and tent the burgers with foil for 3 to 5 minutes.

While the burgers are on the grill or in the oven, set the condiments out in individual bowls.

To serve: Arrange the buns on a platter and place a burger on each bun. Allow guests to dress their own, using the condiments listed here or other Wicked Killer Burger Toppings (pages 32–44). Serve with Glo's Bean Salad on the side.

Glo's Bean Salad

This is Chris's mother, Gloria's, go-to side dish for family barbecues. It is particularly great in the late summer, with farmers' market corn and mint straight from the garden.

2 ears corn, shucked

1 can (15 ounces, 425 g) black beans, rinsed and drained

1 can (15 ounces, 425 g) white beans, rinsed and drained

1 can (15 ounces, 425 g) red kidney beans, rinsed and drained

1 red pepper, seeds removed, cut into ¾-inch (6 mm) dice

4 scallions, minced

1 small red onion, quartered and thinly sliced

1 cucumber, seeds removed, cut into ¾-inch (6 mm) dice

1 ripe but firm avocado, cut into ⅓-inch (8 mm) dice

DRESSING
¾ cup (60 ml) extra-virgin olive oil

2 tablespoons (28 ml) lime juice (from 1 lime)

2 teaspoons (10 ml) red wine vinegar

2 cloves garlic, minced

1 teaspoon (2.5 g) ground cumin

½ cup (48 g) roughly chopped mint

Kosher salt and fresh cracked black pepper, to taste

—
Yield: 2 quarts (2 L)

Grill or broil the corn until it is charred but slightly undercooked. Remove the kernels from the cob and transfer to a large bowl. Add the beans, red pepper, scallions, red onion, cucumber, and avocado.

In a small bowl, whisk the dressing ingredients together. Pour over salad, tossing gently until thoroughly combined. Add the chopped mint and salt and pepper to taste. Cover and refrigerate for at least 1 hour and up to 2 days

Wicked Killer Burger Toppings

We love good mustard, ketchup, mayo, crisp lettuce, and beautiful sliced tomatoes—in season—on our burgers. But sometimes we just can't stop ourselves. When Chris and Andy get together, the gloves come off and everything is a competition. The following toppings are twists on many traditional burger condiments. Mushrooms, onions, and bacon play a big role, but in ways you may not have seen them before, at least not in relation to burgers. And we've thrown in some surprises. When was the last time you had Pickled Green Tops on your burger? It's a delicious combination. But don't just believe us. Try for yourself. In fact, let loose. Mix and match these toppings in whatever way suits your fancy.

Dilled Salmon Roe

2 ounces (55 g) salmon roe

1 tablespoon (5 g) crispy crumbled bacon

1 shallot, peeled and julienned

2 teaspoons (2.6 g) minced fresh dill

—

Yield: About ¾ cup (55 g)

In a small bowl, carefully mix all ingredients together. You don't want to crush any of the roe. Cover and refrigerate for up to 1 hour.

Wicked Killer Burger Toppings

Pig Candy

We learned how to make this during a barbecue contest in Windsor, Vermont. Use real maple syrup and the best thick, smoky slab bacon you can find.

1 cup (225 g) packed light brown sugar

½ teaspoon (0.9 g) cayenne pepper

1 pound (455 g) slab bacon, thick-cut

½ cup (160 g) maple syrup

SPECIAL EQUIPMENT:
Half-sheet pan, cooling racks to fit inside half-sheet pan; or 2 baking sheets with cooling racks to fit inside; disposable gloves

—
Yield: Enough for 4 burgers (and a bit for nibbling)

Preheat the oven to 375°F (190°C, gas mark 5).

In a small bowl, mix the brown sugar and cayenne.

Line a half-sheet pan with aluminum foil and set a cooling rack in the pan. Lay the sliced bacon on the cooling rack. Using your fingers, rub a thick layer of the brown sugar–cayenne mixture into the tops of the bacon slices. Bake for 10 minutes.

Remove from oven and brush each slice with maple syrup. Wearing disposable gloves (the bacon is really hot and sticky at this point), turn the bacon over, sprinkle the remaining brown sugar–cayenne over the second side, and bake for another 10 to 20 minutes or until crispy. Remove and brush with the remaining maple syrup. Cool and serve with burgers of your choice.

Wicked Killer Burger Toppings

Pickled Green Tops

In the spring, we get as many ramps as we can find. We use them in pasta, on steaks, in salads, wherever we can. One of our favorite preparations is pickling them, and since back-yard grilling season and ramp season come close together, we love these on our burgers. You can substitute scallions in this recipe, but they will not yield the same delicate garlic-onion flavor. Serve these whole or give them a rough chop and put them out as a relish.

2 cups (475 ml) white vinegar

2 cups (400 g) sugar

2 cups (475 ml) water

2 tablespoons (30 g) kosher salt

1 tablespoon (3.6 g) plus 1 teaspoon (1.2 g) red pepper flakes

2 teaspoons (4 g) fennel seeds

2 teaspoons (3.6 g) coriander seeds

1 pound (455 g) ramps, roots removed, cleaned (or scallions, if it's not ramp season)

—
Yield: 1½ pints (700 ml)

In a small saucepan over medium heat, bring all the ingredients except the ramps to a boil. Lower the heat and simmer for 2 minutes.

Place the ramps in a large bowl and pour the pickling liquid over them. Cool to room temperature. Transfer the pickled ramps to an airtight jar and refrigerate. These will keep, refrigerated, for up to 1 month.

ESPELETTE AND TOGARASHI PEPPERS

Espelette pepper (piment d'espelette) is a long, red chile pepper grown in France's Basque region. It has an irresistible sweet/smoky/spicy flavor that makes it a perfect complement for meat, Or seafood, or even vegetables.

Togarashi is the Japanese word for red chile pepper. The togarashi blends most commonly available in the United States are usually a combination of powdered or flaked red chile pepper, orange peel, sesame seeds, seaweed, and other ingredients that together range from mild to wicked hot.

Wicked Killer Burger Toppings

Peppered Onion Rings

These rings get their name from the peppers we use to season the onions. Their most distinguishing characteristic, though, is that they are just as good at room temperature as they are hot, so they can be made a day or two before serving.

1 large white onion, peeled and sliced paper thin on a slicer or very sharp mandoline

4 cups (950 ml) buttermilk

1 teaspoon (2 g) plus 1 tablespoon (6 g) ground black pepper, divided

1 teaspoon (1.8 g) plus 1 tablespoon (5.3 g) cayenne pepper, divided

1 teaspoon (2.5 g) plus 1 tablespoon (7 g) smoked paprika (unsmoked is okay, too), divided

Oil, for frying

3 cups (420 g) cornmeal

2 cups (250 g) flour

Kosher salt and fresh cracked black pepper, for seasoning

Espelette or togarashi pepper, for seasoning (see opposite)

SPECIAL EQUIPMENT: Deep fryer, optional

—
Yield: About 6 cups (290 g)

Place the onion slices in a large bowl and pour the buttermilk over them. Season with 1 teaspoon each of the black pepper (2 g), cayenne (1.8 g), and paprika (2.5 g). Toss lightly. Cover and marinate for 4 to 12 hours, refrigerated.

In a deep fryer or deep saucepan, heat oil to 250°F (120°C, gas mark ½).

In a large bowl, mix the remaining tablespoons of black pepper (6 g), cayenne (5.3 g), and paprika (7 g) with the cornmeal and flour. Strain the onions well in a colander, tossing and pressing down on them to remove liquid, and add them all to the dry mixture, tossing and separating until every onion ring is coated and looks dry. Working with a few rings at a time, lift them out of the bowl, shaking off excess coating. Fill the fryer basket half full and cook for 3 to 5 minutes until the rings are just past golden brown. Make sure not to overcrowd, as this will slow down cooking and make the rings greasy.

Remove from the fryer or pan and place on a drying tray lined with paper towel or a paper grocery bag. Immediately season with salt, pepper, and espelette or togarashi pepper. Repeat the process until all the onions are cooked.

Eat immediately or, once cooled, place in an airtight container and store at room temperature for up to 2 days.

Wicked Killer Burger Toppings

Grilled Romaine

Before grilling, make sure to wash the lettuce well. Plunge it into a large bowl of cold water and swish it around, allowing dirt to become dislodged. Remove from water and pat dry.

1 head romaine lettuce, washed, outer leaves removed, and cut in half lengthwise

2 tablespoons (28 ml) olive oil

Kosher salt and fresh cracked black pepper, to taste

1 tablespoon (15 ml) aged sherry vinegar

—

Yield: Topping for 4 burgers, plus a little for a salad

Fill a chimney half full with hardwood lump charcoal and two pieces of newspaper and light. When the flames are just starting to peek through the top of the charcoal, transfer the coals to a kettle grill and let the coals get medium-hot (you should be able to hold your hand above the grill for 10 seconds).

Meanwhile, drizzle olive oil over the lettuce. Season lightly with salt and pepper and place lettuce on grate. Grill for about 3 to 4 minutes or until it starts to wilt and turn brown. Using tongs, turn the lettuce halves over, being careful that the leaves don't separate or the halves don't fall apart. Grill on the other side for 3 to 4 minutes or until wilted and brown.

Remove from the grill, core, cut into chunks, and place in a bowl. Toss the lettuce with vinegar and sprinkle on more salt and pepper to taste. Serve warm on burger.

Spiced and Creamed Shimeji Mushrooms

Shimeji mushrooms are native to East Asia. They grow on trees, in clusters, with long, pale stems. They have a mild, nutty flavor when cooked; the flavor is much stronger when they are raw.

1 tablespoon (15 ml) olive oil

1 tablespoon (14 g) salted butter

1 medium shallot, peeled and julienned

1 pound (455 g) shimeji mushrooms, separated, washed, and dried

2 tablespoons (30 g) sour cream

Kosher salt and fresh cracked black pepper, to taste

1 to 2 teaspoons (2 to 4 g) espelette pepper (see page 38)

In a 12-inch (30 cm) heavy-bottomed sauté pan over medium heat, combine the olive oil and butter and swirl until butter is melted. Add the shallots and cook, stirring occasionally, until the shallots are tender, about 3 to 4 minutes. Add the mushrooms and continue to cook, stirring, for 8 to 10 minutes, until the mushrooms are tender and are starting to brown.

Remove from the pan and transfer to a bowl. Fold in the sour cream and season with salt and pepper to taste. Just before serving, stir in the espelette pepper. Serve warm.

—

Yield: About 2 cups (530 g)

Garlic Confit Jam

1 cup (136 g) garlic cloves, peeled, from 2 to 3 heads
1 sprig fresh thyme
1 cup (235 ml) olive oil
1 cup (235 ml) vegetable oil

—
Yield: Scant ½ cup (160 g)

Preheat oven to 350°F (180°C, gas mark 4).

In a small ovenproof saucepan or Dutch oven, place the garlic, thyme, and both oils. Cover and bake for 45 minutes to 1 hour until the garlic is golden brown and tender.

Remove from the oven. When the cloves are cool enough to handle, squeeze the garlic from the skins into a bowl. Cover and reserve. Pour any remaining oil into a separate bowl and save to brush on burgers or steaks before grilling or use in vinaigrettes.

SMOKING BASICS

- Clean the smoker. Remove any ash or old charcoal from inside the smoker.

- If your smoker does not have a built-in thermometer, place a probe or oven thermometer on the grill grate (see Resources, page 138).

- Fill the charcoal area almost to capacity with unlit lump charcoal.

- Outside the smoker, fill a charcoal chimney with hardwood lump charcoal, crumple two pieces of newspaper and stuff them below the coals, and light the newspaper. Wait for charcoal to become fully ignited.

- Carefully, wearing heatproof gloves, pour the lit charcoal evenly over the bed of unlit charcoal inside the smoker.

- Fill the water pan with cold water.

- Depending on the type of vertical smoker you are using, either close the doors or cover with the smoker lid. Open top and bottom vents completely.

- When the temperature inside the smoker reaches 250°F (120°C, gas mark ½), remove the lid and clean the grill grates with a brush.

- Add food to be cooked and allow the smoker to return to target temperature.

- Close bottom vents by three-quarters.

- Adjust bottom vents to maintain the temperature. Close them slightly to lower temperature; open them slightly to raise temperature.

- If the temperature runs too hot, close the top vent by half. This will bring the temperature down.

- Add water to the water pan every three to four hours. You don't ever want it to run dry.

- A full load of charcoal should be enough fuel for most cooking sessions. But keep an eye on how much charcoal is being used and add more as needed to maintain your target temperature.

Wicked Killer Burger Toppings

Tomato-Ginger Ketchup

2 tablespoons (28 ml) olive oil

1 medium onion, cut into ¾-inch (6 mm) dice

½ cup (48 g) minced fresh ginger (from a 4- to 5-inch [102 to 107 cm] piece)

3 cloves garlic, minced

1 tablespoon (16 g) tamarind paste, dissolved in ½ cup (120 ml) red wine vinegar

¾ cup (60 g) packed brown sugar

1 can (14.5 ounces, 410 g) whole tomatoes, roughly chopped, with juice

Kosher salt and fresh cracked black pepper, to taste

In a heavy-bottomed sauté pan, heat the oil over medium-high heat. Add the onion and cook, stirring occasionally until softened, about 5 minutes. Turn the heat to low and add the ginger and garlic. Continue cooking, stirring occasionally, until the onion is soft and transparent, about 15 minutes.

Turn the heat to medium high and add the vinegar-tamarind mixture and the sugar. Cook, stirring frequently, for 5 minutes, until the mixture is slightly thickened. Add the tomatoes, turn the heat to low, and simmer for 30 minutes. Season with salt and pepper.

—
Yield: Approximately 2 cups (500 g)

Jack D'Or Mustard

Some of the best beers in the world are brewed in New England. One of our favorites, Pretty Things Beer and Ale Project's Jack D'Or, is brewed in Somerville, Massachusetts. It's a simple table beer, perfect to drink anytime. It gives this mustard a slightly spicy flavor, similar to horseradish. Beer and burgers are a perfect match in our book. Thank you, Pretty Things.

1 teaspoon (3 g) mustard powder

1 teaspoon (3 g) garlic powder

3 tablespoons (39 g) sugar

½ teaspoon (2.5 g) kosher salt

1 cup (235 ml) cider vinegar

1 cup (176 g) brown mustard seeds

1 cup (235 ml) Jack D'Or (or other saison/farmhouse ale); save the rest for drinking

—
Yield: 3 cups (750 g)

In a small saucepan set over high heat, bring the mustard powder, garlic powder, sugar, salt, and vinegar to a boil, stirring occasionally. Remove from the heat.

Place the mustard seeds in a small, nonreactive bowl and pour the hot liquid over them. Add the beer and mix well. Cover and refrigerate overnight.

Place the mixture in a food processor fitted with the steel blade and purée, scraping the sides every 30 seconds, for about 3 minutes. The mustard will thicken.

Remove to a jar and refrigerate at least overnight. Mustard will keep, refrigerated, for up to 1 month.

Wicked Killer Burger Toppings

Creamy Garlic Mustard

Before grilling, make sure to wash the lettuce well. Plunge it into a large bowl of cold water and swish it around, allowing dirt to become dislodged. Remove from water and pat dry.

¾ cup (60 ml) olive oil

2 large garlic cloves, minced

¾ cup (175 ml) sherry vinegar

⅓ cup (80 ml) water

1 tablespoon (15 g) packed brown sugar

1 teaspoon (2.2 g) turmeric

2 teaspoons (10 g) kosher salt

½ cup (88 g) mustard seeds, pulsed until cracked

½ cup (115 g) sour cream

—

Yield: About 1½ cups (375 g)

In a small sauté pan, set the oil over medium-high heat. When the oil is hot, add the minced garlic and cook, stirring constantly, until the garlic is brown. Remove from heat and strain, reserving oil for a vinaigrette or other use. Set the browned garlic aside.

In a small saucepan over medium-high heat, bring the sherry vinegar, water, brown sugar, turmeric, and salt to a boil, stirring occasionally. Remove from the heat. Place the mustard seeds in a small, nonreactive bowl and pour the hot liquid over them. Fold in the garlic, cover, and refrigerate for 1 day.

Remove the mustard from the refrigerator and fold in the sour cream. Use immediately or cover and refrigerate until needed, up to 2 weeks.

Triple Crème Stinky Cheese

Soft-ripened cheese, like Brillat-Savarin, Explorateur, and St. André

Ripen cheese at room temperature.

Smear a healthy portion, rind and all, on warm burger bun.

Katie's Burger Buns

Katherine Burchman, the talented pastry chef at Tremont 647, created this recipe, which is in demand at Andy's restaurant for burgers and certain special sandwiches (did we hear somebody mention pulled pork?). They are delicious buns, soft and slightly chewy inside, with a nice crunch outside.

1 cup (235 ml) warm milk (no more than 110°F [43°C])

2 tablespoons (28 ml) warm heavy cream (no more than 110°F [43°C])

1 tablespoon (15 g) packed brown sugar

2 teaspoons (8 g) active dry yeast

3 cups (375 g) flour (all-purpose or bread), plus more for kneading

2 teaspoons (10 g) kosher salt

1 tablespoon (14 g) cold butter

2 eggs, divided

—

Yield: 6 buns

In a small bowl, combine the milk, heavy cream, brown sugar, and yeast and let sit until the mixture becomes foamy, about 10 minutes.

In the bowl of a stand mixer fitted with the whisk attachment, whisk the flour and salt together. With the mixer on low, add the butter. Stir the yeast mixture into the dry ingredients and mix in 1 egg.

Change to the dough hook, increase the speed to medium, and beat the dough until it forms a ball. Sprinkle some flour on a clean counter and knead the dough for 10 to 15 minutes until it is smooth and elastic. Shape the dough into a ball and place it into a well-oiled bowl. Cover with a clean dish towel and let rise in a warm place until doubled in size, 1½ to 2 hours.

Line a baking sheet with a silicone mat or parchment paper.

Divide the dough into six 5-ounce (140 g) pieces and roll each one into a ball. Place the balls on the prepared baking sheet, cover with a clean dish towel, and let the dough rise for another 1½ to 2 hours until it doubles in size.

Preheat the oven to 400°F (200°C, gas mark 6).

Beat the remaining egg and brush the dough balls with the egg wash. Place a shallow pan of water in the bottom of the oven and bake the rolls for 15 minutes or until golden brown.

Flour Bakery Burger Buns

A few years after Andy opened his restaurant, Tremont 647, Joanne Chang, a supremely talented pastry chef, opened Flour Bakery + Cafe a stone's throw away. Renowned for its irresistible pastries and light savory fare, Flour and its owner have garnered national recognition. Many of Flour's deliciously inventive sandwiches are served on these buns, which are also perfect for burgers—and they're vegan, if you care about that sort of thing.

1½ cups (355 ml) water, room temperature

1 teaspoon (4 g) active dry yeast

3 cups (375 g) unbleached all-purpose flour, plus up to about ¾ cup (31 g) more if needed

1 cup (137 g) bread flour

1 tablespoon (13 g) plus 2 teaspoons (9 g) sugar

2 teaspoons (10 g) kosher salt

½ cup (120 ml) olive oil

About ⅛ cup (18 g) cornmeal (one small handful) for the baking sheet

Sesame seeds, optional

—
Yield: 8 buns

In the bowl of a stand mixer fitted with the dough hook attachment, combine the water and yeast and let sit for 20 to 30 seconds to allow the yeast to dissolve. Dump the all-purpose flour, bread flour, sugar, and salt onto the water. Turn the mixer on low speed and let the dough mix for about 30 seconds. (To prevent the flour from flying out of the bowl, you might want to turn the mixer on and off several times until the flour is mixed into the liquid and then keep it on low speed.) When the dough is still shaggy looking, drizzle in the oil, aiming it along the side of the bowl to keep it from splashing and making a mess.

With the mixer still on low speed, knead the dough for 4 to 5 minutes or until it is smooth and supple. The dough should be somewhat sticky but still smooth and have an elastic, stretchy consistency. If it is much stiffer than this, mix in a few tablespoons (45 to 60 ml) water; if it is much looser, add all-purpose flour, 1 tablespoon (8 g) at a time, until it reaches the proper consistency.

Lightly oil a large bowl and transfer the dough to the oiled bowl. Cover the bowl with an oiled piece of plastic wrap or a lint-free cloth. Place the bowl in a warm, draft-free place (78 to 82°F [26 to 28°C] is ideal; an area near the stove or in the oven with only the pilot light on is good) for 2 to 3 hours and let the dough rise until it is about double in bulk.

Sprinkle a large baking sheet with cornmeal.

Using a pastry scraper, divide the dough in half. On a lightly floured surface, shape each half into a rough square, about 4 × 4 inches (10 × 10 cm). Divide each half into 4 equal-size pieces. With lightly floured hands, press/pat each piece into a circle. Bring the edges of the dough into the center so they all meet in the middle. Turn the dough piece over and keep tucking the dough underneath so you have a little tight ball of dough.

Bring edges of dough into center.

Turn dough over onto lightly floured surface.

Tuck dough underneath to form tight ball.

Continue tucking and turning dough.

When dough is formed, transfer to a baking sheet.

Place the ball of dough on the prepared baking sheet and repeat with the other 7 pieces of dough. Sprinkle the dough balls with flour and lightly cover with a lint-free cloth or oiled plastic wrap and place in a warm area (78 to 80°F [26 to 27°C] is ideal) for about 2 hours or until dough is doubled in size and soft.

Preheat oven to 400°F (200°C, gas mark 6) and place rack in center of oven.

Remove the cloth/plastic wrap. Sprinkle the rolls with a little more flour and slap them flat with the palm of your hand to deflate the dough. Sprinkle evenly with sesame seeds, if desired. Place in oven and bake for 15 to 20 minutes until rolls are golden brown. Remove and let cool.

These buns are best on the day they are made. You can serve them up to 2 days later, reheated for a few minutes in a 350°F (180°C, gas mark 4) oven.

Burgers 101

CHAPTER 3

New American Classics

At his restaurant, Tremont 647, Andy has always been at the forefront of American cuisine. And traveling the country to compete on the barbecue circuit, Andy and Chris have not only mastered what some call our only true native cuisine, but have been sampling the fare from coast to coast for many years. In this chapter, we wanted to incorporate these experiences, along with influences of chefs we know from our own city and others we've visited, into some really fun burgers that are destined to become new classics.

The Hill Country Brisket Burger grew out of our time traveling to competitions. We developed the brat burger to complement James Beard Award-winning pastry chef Mindy Segal's Pretzel Buns and Pepper Jack Cheese Sauce. The Schlow Burger is a contribution from one of our favorite Boston chefs, Michael Schlow.

Brat Burger

When Mindy Segal, one of our favorite pastry chefs, a James Beard Award winner, and owner of Mindy's Bakery in Chicago, offered us her bun and sauce recipes, we couldn't say no. They are just too good. After several discussions about the best type of burger to serve with them, basically, it came down to, "What goes best with pretzels and cheese?" Chris came up with the idea of a Brat Burger. It was such a natural that we couldn't believe we ever had to think about it. We heart you, Mindy. Thanks.

12 ounces (340 g) ground veal

12 ounces (340 g) ground pork

1 teaspoon (2.2 g) freshly ground nutmeg

1½ teaspoons (3 g) fresh cracked white pepper, plus more to taste

1½ teaspoons (2.7 g) ginger powder

1 tablespoon (15 ml) Hefeweizen beer (drink the rest)

1 tablespoon (14 g) butter, softened

2 teaspoons (10 g) kosher salt, plus more to taste

Vegetable oil, for cooking

4 Mindy's Pretzel Buns (recipe follows)

Mindy's Pepper Jack Cheese Sauce (recipe follows)

—
Yield: 4 burgers

In a large bowl, combine the veal, pork, nutmeg, 1½ teaspoons (3 g) white pepper, ginger powder, beer, butter, and 2 teaspoons (10 g) salt.

Divide the mixture into four 6-ounce (170 g) portions and shape into burgers according to the technique in chapter 1 (page 13). Refrigerate, covered, while you prepare the skillet.

Heat a skillet over high heat until very hot. If you have an infrared thermometer, the skillet should register at least 500°F (250°C). Or test by brushing on a bit of oil. When the skillet starts to smoke, it is ready.

Brush oil onto the skillet and remove the burgers from the refrigerator. Season the burgers with salt and white pepper and sear them for 2 minutes. Flip the burgers and cook for another 2 minutes. Transfer to a plate and let rest, tented, for 5 minutes.

While the burgers are resting, heat the cheese sauce.

To serve: Place the burgers on the bottoms of the buns and spoon the cheese on top. Place the tops of the buns over the cheese.

Mindy's Pretzel Buns

2½ teaspoons (10 g)
dry instant yeast

½ cup (120 ml) buttermilk

¾ cup (60 ml) pale ale

¾ cup (175 ml) hot water

3¾ cups (514 g) bread flour,
plus up to ½ cup (69 g)
more as needed

1 tablespoon (15 g) plus
1 teaspoon (5 g) kosher salt

1 teaspoon (4 g) sugar

¾ cup (60 g) packed
light brown sugar

2 tablespoons (28 ml)
vegetable oil, for brushing

BAKING SODA BATH
1 gallon (4 L) water

½ cup (120 ml) pale ale

⅓ cup (75 g) packed
light brown sugar

⅓ cup (74 g) baking soda

—
Yield: 8 buns

In the bowl of a stand mixer fitted with the dough hook, dissolve the yeast in buttermilk, beer, and water.

Add the 3¾ cups (514 g) flour, 1 tablespoon (15 g) salt, and sugars and mix on low speed until a loose dough forms. With the machine still running, slowly drizzle in the vegetable oil. When the dough is completely combined, stop the mixer and scrape the sides of the bowl with a spatula.

Turn the mixer to medium-high speed and work the dough for 7 to 10 minutes until it is smooth and elastic. If the dough is too wet/sticky, you may need to add more flour, 1 tablespoon (9 g) at a time.

Spray a large bowl with nonstick cooking oil or wipe with oil and place dough inside. Cover with a clean dish towel. Let the dough rise at room temperature for about 4 hours until doubled in volume.

Turn the dough out onto a clean counter. Fold the dough in half twice and let rise in the refrigerator for about 2 more hours or until doubled in volume again.

Shortly before the dough has finished its second rise, prepare the baking soda bath. In a 6-quart (6 L) saucepot, bring the water, ale, brown sugar, and baking soda to a rolling boil.

Preheat the oven to 350°F (180°C, gas mark 4). Spray a sheet pan with nonstick cooking oil.

Turn the dough out onto a floured counter and divide into eight 5-ounce (140 g) pieces. Roll each piece into a ball.

Working one at a time, poach each ball in the baking soda bath for 15 seconds and then flip it and poach for 15 more seconds. Transfer to the prepared sheet pan.

Brush the buns with vegetable oil and sprinkle with the remaining teaspoon (5 g) of salt. Bake for about 14 minutes, turning halfway through, until they are golden brown.

Mindy's Pepper Jack Cheese Sauce

1 cup (235 ml) heavy whipping cream

6 slices white American cheese

½ cup (4 ounces, 115 g) shredded pepper Jack cheese

2 tablespoons (28 ml) fresh lemon juice

Kosher salt to taste

—

Yield: About 2 cups (485 g)

In a 2-quart (2 L) saucepot over medium heat, bring the cream to a light simmer. Whisk in the cheeses until they are fully melted and smooth. Season with lemon juice and salt to taste. Reserve until ready to use.

Hill Country Brisket Burger

We cook a lot of brisket on the barbecue competition trail, and we always save our trimmings. In fact, some of our favorite recipes have come from the creative use of trimmings. We freeze the odd, leftover pieces of brisket, and when we have enough, we make this awesome burger. You don't have to wait until you accumulate enough scraps, though.

1½ pounds (680 g) brisket flat, trimmed of excess fat

1½ pounds (680 g) brisket point, trimmed of excess fat

6 tablespoons (38 g) Basic BBQ Rub (recipe follows)

1 cup (250 g) Pit Sauce (recipe follows)

12 slices inexpensive white sandwich bread

Garlic Butter (recipe follows)

1 batch Quick-Pickled Onions (recipe follows)

SPECIAL EQUIPMENT: Grinder attachment to stand mixer

—
Yield: 6 burgers

Freeze the brisket until stiff but not frozen, about 1 hour.

Using the coarse grinder plate, grind the brisket according to the technique in chapter 1 (page 13). Refrigerate until ready to use.

Prepare a kettle grill for two-zone grilling (see pages 15–16). Clean the grill grate well with a stiff wire brush. Build a hot charcoal fire on one side. Leave the other side empty. This provides a cooler zone to finish cooking the burger.

While the grill is heating, prepare the patties. Shape the ground beef into 6 square patties that are slightly larger than the bread and a little thicker around the edges than in the center—about 1 inch (2.5 cm) on the edges and ¾ inch (2 cm) in the middle. The center of the burger will expand during the cooking process and result in an even thickness. Don't overwork the meat or pack it tightly. The loose consistency may make the grilling process bit more challenging, but it yields a super-tender burger.

Sprinkle 1 tablespoon (6 g) Basic BBQ Rub on both sides of each patty. Grill 2 minutes per side, uncovered. Carefully move patties to the cool side of the grill, baste generously with Pit Sauce, and cover the grill. Let patties cook 2 to 3 minutes for rare ($125°F, 52°C$) internal temperature), 3 to 4 minutes for medium rare ($130°F, 54°C$), or 4 to 5 minutes for medium ($135°F, 57°C$).

Remove the burgers from the grill and rest on a platter, loosely tented with foil.

Lay the bread slices on the grill just long enough to get a light char, a minute or so. Using tongs, turn the bread over and char the other side. Remove and brush 1 side of each slice with softened garlic butter.

Place a patty on one buttered piece of toast, heap generously with onions, and lay another piece of toast on top. Slice in half. Repeat for the remaining burgers. Serve with lots of napkins.

New American Classics 55

Basic BBQ Rub

2 tablespoons (30 g) kosher salt

2 tablespoons (14 g) paprika

1 tablespoon (6 g) fresh cracked black pepper

1 tablespoon (7.5 g) chili powder

1 teaspoon (3 g) granulated garlic

1 teaspoon (2.4 g) granulated onion

—

Yield: ½ cup (150 g)

In a small bowl, combine all ingredients and mix well. Store in an airtight container for up to 1 month.

Pit Sauce

2 cups (480 g) ketchup

½ cup (120 ml) Worcestershire sauce

½ cup (120 ml) cider vinegar

¾ cup (60 ml) water

2 tablespoons (13 g) Basic BBQ Rub (recipe above)

1 tablespoon (15 ml) chipotle hot sauce

1 clove garlic, minced

—

Yield: 3 cups (430 g)

Combine all ingredients in a saucepan and simmer gently, whisking occasionally, for 30 minutes.

Garlic Butter

½ cup (1 stick, 112 g) unsalted butter, room temperature

2 cloves garlic, minced

1 tablespoon (4 g) minced fresh parsley

1 teaspoon (5 ml) Worcestershire sauce

1 teaspoon (2 g) finely chopped lemon zest

Pinch of kosher salt

Pinch of fresh cracked black pepper

—
Yield: ½ cup (112 g)

In a medium-size bowl, mix the ingredients thoroughly with a rubber spatula. Cover with plastic and refrigerate. Bring to room temperature before spreading on toast.

Quick-Pickled Onions

1 medium red onion, sliced very thin

1 teaspoon (1.8 g) coriander seeds, toasted and ground

½ teaspoon (1 g) cumin seeds, toasted and ground

¾ teaspoon (0.3 g) red pepper flakes

¾ cup (60 ml) cider vinegar

2 tablespoons (28 ml) water

1 tablespoon (13 g) sugar

Pinch of kosher salt

—
Yield: About 1½ cups (315 g) onions

Place the onion slices in a medium, stainless steel mixing bowl. Add the coriander, cumin, and red pepper flakes and toss to distribute.

In a small saucepan over medium heat, bring the vinegar and water to a boil. Add the sugar and stir until dissolved. Remove from the heat and pour over the onions. Mix well and season with a generous pinch of salt. Let cool to room temperature. Transfer to a jar and refrigerate for up to 1 week.

Tortilla-Wrapped New Mexican Chile Burger

Don't knock it 'til you've tried it. The first time we served this burger at a party, the jokes were flying. A burger in a bun, wrapped in a tortilla? "The Carb Burger," people called it. Then they started eating, and nobody was joking any more. We're not recommending that you eat like this every day. All we can say is, it's even better than it looks. And if you have any relish left over, enjoy it with your morning eggs.

GREEN CHILE RELISH

2 New Mexican green chiles (or poblano chiles), roasted, peeled, seeded, stemmed, and roughly chopped

¾ medium red onion, diced

1 tablespoon (1 g) chopped fresh cilantro

1½ teaspoons (7.5 ml) fresh lime juice

¾ teaspoon (4 ml) extra-virgin olive oil

½ clove garlic, peeled and minced

½ teaspoon (0.6 g) red pepper flakes

Kosher salt and fresh cracked black pepper, to taste

BURGERS

1½ pounds (680 g) ground chuck, or chuck for grinding

1 teaspoon (2.1 g) cumin seeds, toasted and ground

2 tablespoons (13 g) New Mexico Chile Ground (see Resources, page 138)

continued

Make the green chile relish: In a small bowl, mix together the New Mexican chiles, red onion, cilantro, lime juice, olive oil, garlic, and red pepper flakes. Season with salt and pepper. Set aside until the burgers are ready.

Make the burgers: If you are grinding the meat, mix the chuck with the cumin and chili powder and grind according to the technique in chapter 1 (page 13). If you have ground meat, add the spices and mix thoroughly. Shape the burgers according to the technique in chapter 1 (see page 13).

Heat a skillet over high heat until very hot. If you have an infrared thermometer, the skillet should register at least 500°F (250°C). Or test by brushing on a bit of oil. When the skillet starts to smoke, it is ready.

Brush oil onto the skillet and sear the burgers for 2 minutes per side. Skip the resting step. Instead, remove the burgers from the heat and transfer to a sheet pan. Quickly spread about 2 tablespoons (30 g) of Green Chile Relish on each one and quickly top with 2 slices of cheese. Let the burgers rest on the pan for a minute so the cheese sets.

Fill a saucepan (or Windsor pan) with 4 inches (10 cm) of oil and heat to 350°F (180°C, gas mark 4).

continued

Quick and Easy Burger Cookbook

Spread Green Chile Relish on bun.

Top with two slices of cheese.

Invert burger, in its bun, onto center of a tortilla.

Wrap tortilla around burger.

Make overlapping folds.

Result should look something like a pentagon.

Use eggwash to hold down each fold.

Place burgers in pan, fold-side down.

Fry for 2 minutes per side.

Tortilla-Wrapped New Mexican Chile Burger (continued)

Kosher salt and fresh cracked black pepper, to taste

Oil for frying

8 slices pepper Jack cheese or your favorite cheese

4 burger buns, toasted

4 twelve-inch (30 cm) flour tortillas

1 egg mixed with 1 tablespoon (15 ml) water, for tortilla wraps

—

Yield: 4 burgers

While the oil is heating, wrap the burgers. Place each burger in a bun. One at a time, invert the burger, in its bun, onto the center of a tortilla and wrap the tortilla around it, making overlapping folds and using egg wash to hold down each fold. The result should look something like a pentagon.

Place burgers in the pan, fold side down. Fry for about 2 minutes per side until the tortillas are evenly browned and crispy. Serve immediately with green chile relish.

Josh Ozersky's Favorite Burger

It's no exaggeration to say that Josh Ozersky was something of an expert on burgers. He literally wrote the book on the subject—*The Hamburger: A History*. His favorite burger, which is really saying something, comes from Jose Soto, who was the grill cook at the now-defunct White Diamond, a slider joint in Linden, New Jersey. Ozersky managed to coax the recipe, which owes as much to the technique as the ingredients, out of Soto, and made it his own. Then he shared it with us. Josh said the recipe is "simple, but it isn't easy, because it has to be done quickly, so it may need some practice." The sliders are cooked individually, and Josh warned that each one gets a little harder to cook because the pan becomes messier. You should find, however, that the results are well worth any difficulty.

5 slices American deli-style cheese, halved, room temperature

10 white, unseeded, soft white supermarket dinner rolls, split in half horizontally

1 pound (455 g) fresh ground chuck, 80/20 or 70/30 meat-to-fat ratio (Josh preferred 70/30)

1 large yellow onion (you can use a red onion if you like)

Kosher salt to taste

Oil, for cooking

Condiments of your choice

—

Yield: 10 sliders

Arrange the individual cheese slices and open the buns on a platter or cutting board near your cooking surface. Once the burgers start to cook, you will need them quickly.

Divide the meat into 10 even portions. Roll each one into a meatball about the size of a ping-pong ball.

Dice the onion medium-fine and place in a small bowl. Add warm salted water just to cover and set beside the stove.

Heat a skillet over high heat until very hot. If you have an infrared thermometer, the skillet should register at least 500°F (250°C). Or test by brushing on a bit of oil. When the skillet starts to smoke, it is ready.

While the skillet is heating, working one at a time, flatten a meatball slightly and sprinkle it liberally on both sides with kosher salt. Salt drives much of this recipe.

Brush oil onto the skillet and place the flattened ball on it. Just after it hits the pan, flip it over and using a solid, reinforced metal spatula, press hard to flatten it. You want it really thin. Do this just once, while the meat is still cold.

After the burger has sizzled for about 30 to 40 seconds, top with about a tablespoon (15 g) of the watery onions. This will produce a good amount of onion fumes. That's okay. Spread the water and onions as evenly as you can and press them gently into the meat; don't squish down hard.

Wait another 30 seconds and taking great care to lift the meat from the pan with its crust intact, flip it over. Immediately put a slice of cheese on the meat and a bottom bun on top of the cheese. Wait another 10 to 15 seconds and remove onto a top bun.

Invert onto serving platter and repeat to make 10 sliders. Serve with condiments of your choice.

New American Classics

Homage to Island Creek Oysters Burger

We are lucky to live near the ocean and even luckier to live near Island Creek Oysters in Duxbury, where Skip Bennett and his team grow some of the best oysters in the United States. We've always loved the combination of sweet and briny oysters paired with rich, succulent meat, especially pork. To us, this is the ultimate surf-and-turf combo, perfect for summer—or anytime, really.

12 ounces (340 g) ground pork

12 ounces (340 g) ground beef chuck

1 teaspoon (0.8 g) minced fresh sage leaves

2 teaspoons (2.4 g) crushed red pepper flakes

Kosher salt and fresh cracked black pepper, to taste for seasoning

4 leaves Bibb lettuce

Tartar Aioli (recipe follows)

8 pieces bacon, crispy

Fried Oysters (recipe follows)

4 Katie's Burger Buns, toasted (page 45)

—

Yield: 4 burgers

In a large bowl, combine the ground pork and beef with the sage and red pepper flakes. Season with salt and pepper. Divide the meat into four 6-ounce (170 g) portions and shape into patties according to the technique in chapter 1 (see page 13).

We prefer the griddle/skillet technique to cook these burgers, but grilling works very well, too, especially in the summer. If using the skillet, heat it over high heat until very hot. If you have an infrared thermometer, the skillet should register at least 500°F (250°C). Or test by brushing on a bit of oil. When the skillet starts to smoke, it is ready.

While the skillet is heating, prepare the oyster coating and a deep saucepan for frying. Fill with 4 inches (10 cm) of oil and set over medium-high heat. The oil should reach 350°F (180°C) by the time you are ready to fry the oysters.

Brush oil onto the skillet and sear the burgers for 2 minutes. Turn the burgers over and cook for another 2 minutes. Transfer to a plate, tent with foil, and let the burgers rest for 5 minutes.

If grilling, prepare a kettle grill for two-zone grilling (see pages 15–16). Clean the grill grate well with a stiff wire brush. Build a hot charcoal fire on one side. Leave the other side empty. Brush the grill grate with oil.

Place the burgers on the grill directly over the fire and cook for 2 minutes. Turn the burgers over and cook for another 2 minutes. Move to the cool side of the grill and cook, covered, for 5 minutes.

While the burgers are resting or cooking on the cool side of the grill, fry the oysters.

To serve: Place a piece of Bibb lettuce on the bottom of each bun. Spread a generous schmear of Tartar Aioli on the top half. Set the burgers on the lettuce and top with two slices of bacon, 3 oysters, and the top bun. Eat immediately.

New American Classics

Fried Oysters

You can use any oysters you like, but we prefer medium to large ones here. If you don't want to put 3 oysters on your burger, it's always fun to have a few extras for munching.

2 cups (275 g) cornmeal

1 cup (125 g) flour

½ teaspoon (0.9 g) cayenne pepper

½ teaspoon (0.7 g) dried thyme

½ teaspoon (1 g) ground black pepper

12 Island Creek Oysters (if you can get them, or your favorites), shucked, meats only

Vegetable oil, for frying

Kosher salt, for seasoning

—
Yield: 12 oysters

In a small bowl, mix together the cornmeal, flour, cayenne pepper, thyme, and black pepper. Fill a large sauté pan with ½ inch (1 cm) of oil and set over high heat. Bring the oil to 350°F (180°C).

Toss the oysters in the dry mixture to coat completely and shake lightly to remove excess.

Carefully place the oysters in the pan. Fry for 30 seconds per side, turning carefully with a slotted spoon or spider, until golden brown and not entirely firm. Remove from the pan and transfer to a paper towel-lined plate. Season lightly with kosher salt.

Tartar Aioli

1 egg

1 tablespoon (15 ml) fresh lemon juice

2 tablespoons (30 g) minced dill pickles

1 tablespoon (15 ml) plus 1 teaspoon (5 ml) dill pickle juice

2 teaspoons (10 g) Dijon mustard

2 teaspoons (4.7 g) Old Bay Seasoning

1¾ cups (295 ml) canola or vegetable oil

2 teaspoons (9 g) sugar

Kosher salt and fresh cracked black pepper, to taste

—
Yield: 1½ cups (345 g)

In the bowl of a food processor fitted with the steel blade, combine the egg, lemon juice, pickles, pickle juice, mustard, and Old Bay Seasoning. Process until smooth.

With the motor still running, slowly drizzle the oil into the food processor until the mixture is smooth, thick, and shiny, with the consistency of mayonnaise. Stir in the sugar and salt and pepper to taste. Refrigerate, covered, for up to 1 week.

Quick and Easy Burger Cookbook

Belted Cow Bistro Veal Parmigiana Burger

John Delpha, chef-owner of the now-closed Belted Cow Bistro in Essex Junction, Vermont, is not only one of our favorite chefs, but he happens to be our barbecue teammate. We have never tried anything of his that we didn't love, so when he offered one of his burger recipes for this book, we were honored. John uses local veal for this burger. We recommend you do the same.

The recipe makes 8 burgers, which is more than you will need for the parmigiana sandwiches. In our experience, the burgers are so delicious even without the fixin's that people fight over them all by themselves. But if you don't want to shape the additional meat into patties, John suggests rolling it into meatballs, baking it on a sheet in a 400°F (200°C, gas mark 6) oven, and if you can resist eating them all right away, freezing them. (We know, this is a burger book, but we're nothing if not flexible.)

---

1 onion, finely diced

4 cloves garlic, chopped

¾ cup (60 ml) olive oil

Kosher salt and fresh cracked black pepper, to taste

2 pounds (900 g) ground veal (grass- and milk-fed recommended)

¾ cup (5 g) dried parsley flakes

1¾ cups (63 g) panko

⅓ cup (80 ml) heavy cream

¾ cup (75 g) grated Parmesan, divided

3 eggs

Oil, for cooking

1⅓ cups (327 g) Tomato Sauce (recipe follows)

4 ounces (115 g) fresh provolone, cut into 4 slices

4 ounces (115 g) fresh mozzarella, cut into 4 slices

4 sandwich buns or kaiser rolls

Basil Pesto (recipe follows)

—

Yield: 4 Veal Parmigiana Burgers, with extra left over for plain burgers or meatballs

In a large, covered sauté pan over medium heat, sweat the onions and garlic in oil with salt and pepper. Lift the lid to stir, occasionally, until vegetables are soft and onions are translucent, about 10 minutes.

In a large bowl, combine the veal, parsley flakes, panko, heavy cream, ½ cup (50 g) Parmesan, and eggs. Stir in onions and squeeze the mixture together with your hands. Divide the mixture evenly into 8 portions and shape into patties according to the technique in chapter 1 (see page 13).

We like to cook these burgers in a cast-iron skillet on a kettle grill because it gives the meat a great sear and crust while adding a little dimension of smokiness. Build a fire in a kettle grill (pages 15–16). When the fire is hot (you can't hold your hands over it for more than 5 seconds), heat a cast-iron skillet on the grate. Rub the patties with oil, season with salt and pepper, and sear in pan for 4 minutes. Flip the patties and sear for another 4 minutes. Cover each patty with ⅓ cup (82 g) of Tomato Sauce, close the grill, and cook for 4 minutes. Open the grill, top the burgers with provolone, mozzarella, and remaining ¾ cup (25 g) Parmesan, and close for another 2 minutes to melt the cheese. Remove the pan from the grill and transfer the burgers to a plate to rest, tented with foil.

If you want to cook these indoors, use the basic griddle/skillet method in chapter 1 (see pages 14–15). Before you begin, preheat oven to 400°F (200°C, gas mark 6). Heat a skillet over high heat until very hot. If you have an infrared thermometer, the skillet

continued

New American Classics 67

Belted Cow Bistro Veal Parmigiana Burger (continued)

should register at least 500°F (250°C). Or test by brushing on a bit of oil. When the skillet starts to smoke, it is ready.

Brush oil onto the skillet and sear the burgers for 2 minutes. Transfer to a baking pan and cover each patty with ⅓ cup (82 g) of Tomato Sauce. Bake for 5 minutes. Remove from the oven and top with provolone, mozzarella, and the remaining ¾ cup (25 g) Parmesan and return to oven for about 2 minutes or until cheese melts.

To serve: Toast the buns, if desired. Brush Basil Pesto on insides of buns. Place patties on the bottom half, top with the other half, and serve.

Basil Pesto

2 cups (80 g) packed fresh basil leaves, stems removed

2 cloves garlic, sliced

8 ounces (225 g) Parmigiano-Reggiano, cut into chunks

2 tablespoons (18 g) pine nuts

¾ cup (175 ml) olive oil

—

Yield: 1½ cups (390 g)

In the bowl of a food processor fitted with the steel blade, process all ingredients except the oil until combined. With the motor running, add the oil through the feed tube and process until smooth.

Tomato Sauce

⅓ cup (80 ml) olive oil

6 cloves garlic, sliced thin

1 can (28 ounces, 785 g) tomatoes, preferably San Marzano, crushed by hand

Kosher salt to taste

—

Yield: 2½ cups (610 g)

In a 2-quart (2 L) saucepan, combine the oil and garlic. Place the pan over medium heat and bring to a simmer. Cook, stirring often, until the garlic is dark golden, about 5 minutes, watching closely so the garlic doesn't burn. Add the tomatoes and bring to a simmer. Adjust the heat so the mixture simmers gently until thickened, stirring occasionally, about 30 minutes. Season liberally with salt. Remove from the heat and reserve.

Pastrami Burger

When we're not hanging out at BBQ joints, we devote our time to burger stands and Jewish delis. In this burger, we bring together the key elements of a great pastrami sandwich and a perfectly cooked patty. Eat up!

1½ pounds (680 g) beef chuck or ground chuck

½ teaspoon (2.5 g) kosher salt

8 slices pastrami

1 cup (142 g) sauerkraut

2 tablespoons (28 ml) sauerkraut liquid

4 slices Swiss cheese

Softened butter, for toasting

8 slices rye bread

Russian Dressing (recipe follows)

—
Yield: 4 burgers

Preheat oven to 300°F (150°C, gas mark 2).

If grinding, cut the beef into strips and freeze until stiff, about 45 minutes. Salt the beef. Using the coarse grinder plate, grind according to the technique in chapter 1 (page 13). If using ground chuck, mix with salt before shaping.

Divide into 4 equal portions and shape into rectangles roughly the size of the bread and about ½ inch (1 cm) thick.

Heat a skillet over high heat until very hot. If you have an infrared thermometer, the skillet should register at least 500°F (250°C). Or test by brushing on a bit of oil. When the skillet starts to smoke, it is ready.

Cook the patties for 2 minutes. Flip and cook for 1 minute more. Transfer the patties to a baking sheet.

Sauté the pastrami slices on the skillet for 1 minute. Place on top of the burgers. Sauté the sauerkraut and 2 tablespoons (28 ml) reserved liquid for 1 to 2 minutes. Spoon some sauerkraut on top of each burger. Lay a slice of Swiss cheese over each burger and place the baking sheet in the oven just until the cheese melts, about 1 minute.

To serve: Wipe the skillet clean. Brush both sides of the bread with softened butter. Toast the bread in the skillet until it just begins to color. With a spatula, place each burger on a slice of toast. Schmear Russian dressing liberally on the other slices of toast, place on top of the burgers, and serve.

Russian Dressing

¾ cup (175 g) mayonnaise

¾ cup (60 g) sour cream

3 tablespoons (45 g) ketchup

2 tablespoons (30 g) pickle relish

1 tablespoon (15 g) prepared horseradish, drained

1 teaspoon (5 ml) Worcestershire sauce

1 teaspoon (5 ml) hot sauce

1 teaspoon (4 g) sugar

Pinch salt and pepper

In a small bowl, mix all ingredients together well. Cover and refrigerate for up to 2 weeks.

—

Yield: 1½ cups (365 g)

Diner-Style Steamed Cheeseburgers

We love it when we go to a diner and see the cooks using a hubcap as a cooktop cover. We know we're in a really greasy-spoon place and the burgers are going to be great. Happily, you don't have to be in a diner to eat diner food.

These thin burgers cook rather quickly. We recommend cooking them on a skillet, and a metal pie pan works well if you don't have a clean hubcap lying around. This method isn't as much about the sear as about keeping the patties juicy and moist.

1 pound (455 g) ground beef or chuck

8 slices your favorite cheese

Oil for skillet

Kosher salt and fresh cracked black pepper, to taste

Your favorite Wicked Killer Burger Toppings (pages 32–44)

2 burger buns, toasted if you like

SPECIAL EQUIPMENT: Metal pie tin, 12-inch (30 cm) skillet lid, or hubcap; 1 squeeze bottle filled with water

—

Yield: 2 double cheeseburgers

Divide the beef into 4 equal portions and shape according to the technique in chapter 1 (see page 13), but make 4-ounce (115 g) instead of 6-ounce (170 g) balls. Season with salt and pepper.

Heat a skillet over high heat until very hot. If you have an infrared thermometer, the skillet should register at least 500°F (250°C). Or test by brushing on a bit of oil. When the skillet starts to smoke, it is ready.

Brush the oil onto the skillet and arrange 2 burgers close together. Cover with a pie tin or hubcap and let set for 30 seconds. Using a spatula, lift the cover slightly and squirt some water on the hot surface—not the burgers—and quickly cover again. This helps the burgers cook faster and keeps them super juicy.

Cook for 30 seconds more, remove the cover, flip the burgers, and top with cheese. Cover again, squirt some more water, and then let cook for 1 minute more or until desired doneness. Transfer the burgers to a plate and tent with foil. Repeat cooking with remaining 2 burgers.

To serve: Place 2 burgers on each bun and serve with your favorite Wicked Killer Burger Toppings.

continued

New American Classics

Diner-Style Steamed Cheeseburgers *(continued)*

After flipping, top burgers with cheese.

Squirt some water onto the cooking surface.

Ready for tasting

The Schlow Burger

Our friend Michael Schlow, chef-owner of several renowned New England restaurants, created this burger, which he serves at his flagship, Radius. It has practically taken on a life of its own since taking top honors at the 2008 South Beach Wine & Food Festival Burger Bash. Some people dream about the horseradish/mayonnaise/lemon sauce. Others can't get enough of the crispy onions on top. Most just love the way the whole thing comes together perfectly. Michael generously shared his recipe with us.

BURGERS
18 ounces (510 g) ground beef (ask the butcher for 80 percent lean)

2 tablespoons (28 ml) extra-virgin olive oil

Kosher salt and fresh cracked black pepper, to taste

SAUCE
4 tablespoons (60 g) mayonnaise

2 teaspoons (10 g) prepared white horseradish

Juice of ½ lemon

Fresh cracked black pepper, to taste

2 thick slices good-quality Vermont or English Cheddar

2 large hamburger buns, split in half (Flour Bakery, page 46, or Brioche, page 136)

Crispy Onions (recipe follows)

Note: The sauce can be made up to three days ahead. The onions can be prepared early on the day they will be served.

—
Yield: 2 burgers

In a large bowl, mix the ground beef with the olive oil, salt, and pepper.

Divide the meat into two 9-ounce (255 g) portions and shape into patties. Refrigerate until the grill is ready (do not do this more than an hour in advance).

Prepare a kettle grill for two-zone grilling (see page 16). Clean the grill grate well with a stiff wire brush. Build a hot charcoal fire on one side. Leave the other side empty. This provides a cooler zone to finish cooking the burger.

While the grill is heating, in a small bowl, mix the mayonnaise, horseradish, and lemon juice and season with black pepper. Cover and refrigerate until ready to serve.

Five to 7 minutes before you are ready to cook, take the burgers out of the refrigerator.

Brush the grill with oil. Place the burgers on the grate and cook for 1½ minutes (for rare). Give the burgers a quarter-turn to "mark" them and cook 1½ more minutes. Flip the burgers over and cook for another 1½ minutes. Rotate a quarter-turn to "mark" the other side and cook for 1½ minutes longer.

Transfer the burgers to the cool side of the grill and cover each one with a slice of cheese. Cover the grill and cook the burgers for 4 minutes. Toast the buns, if desired.

To serve: Place a burger on each bun. Spread plenty of the horseradish sauce on each burger; it should drip down the sides. Top with Crispy Onions and season with fresh cracked black pepper. Slather more sauce on the other half of the bun and place it on top of the burger.

New American Classics 75

Crispy Onions

1 large yellow onion, sliced into ⅓- to ½-inch (8 mm to 1 cm) thick rings

2 cups (475 ml) canola oil

—

Yield: About ½ cup (110 g), enough for 2 Schlow Burgers

In a small saucepan over high heat, bring the onion rings and oil to boil. Reduce the heat so the onions are gently frying.

Turn the onions with a fork every 30 seconds or so and cook until they turn golden brown, 12 to 15 minutes. If the onions are not golden brown in 15 minutes, increase the heat.

Remove the onions from the oil and arrange in a single layer on paper towels or a paper shopping bag. (At this point they won't be crispy, but after a few minutes, as the caramelized sugars cool and harden, the onions will become deliciously crisp.)

CHAPTER 4

Where's the Beef?

When we started writing this book, we knew we wanted to expand beyond beef burgers and create options for vegetarians, pescatarians, and anyone else looking for something a little different. The Beet Burger is completely vegan—and we weren't even trying for that. Served on Flour Bakery Burger Buns, it makes a vegan sandwich. But we suggest blindfolding your carnivorous friends and feeding them a Beet Burger. We doubt they'll ever suspect it doesn't contain any meat. Again, we weren't even trying.

For people who love beef burgers but want something a little leaner, we offer two bison options. Our Salmon Burger makes delicious use of a little-used part of this beautiful fish—the belly. Lamb Juicy Lucy is a play on inside-out cheeseburgers. And the 647's Breakfast Burger, featuring a sausage patty on an English muffin, would make Jimmy Dean proud. Serve it to your family and it will make them proud—and happy.

Salmon Burger

The key to this burger is using belly. Your fishmonger will probably be thrilled to sell it to you because customers usually gravitate to more popular steaks and fillets. But in our opinion the belly is the best part of the fish. It is used a lot for salmon tartare, but we like it for burgers, too, because it is the fattiest part of the fish. In addition to being incredibly flavorful, it will stay juicy when it is cooked.

2½ pounds (1.1 kg) salmon belly

1 tablespoon (15 ml) soy sauce

1 teaspoon (5 g) Dijon mustard

2 cloves garlic, minced

¾ cup (15 g) minced
fresh parsley

1 egg

1½ cups (75 g) panko

Kosher salt to taste

2 tablespoons (28 ml)
vegetable oil, for cooking

½ lemon

6 Katie's Burger Buns (page 45)
or Brioche Buns (page 136)

Dill Mayonnaise (recipe follows)

Arugula for garnish

2 tablespoons (30 g) crème
fraîche, for garnish

1 tablespoon (3 g) minced
chives, for garnish

Dilled Salmon Roe (page 32),
optional

—
Yield: 6 burgers

Cut 2 pounds (900 g) of the salmon into strips and place in the freezer until stiff, about 20 minutes.

Roughly chop the remaining ½ pound (225 g) of salmon.

Remove the salmon from the freezer and grind, using the coarse or medium grind plate, according to the technique in chapter 1 (see page 13). If you do not have a grinder, place in the bowl of a food processor fitted with the chopping blade and pulse until coarsely ground.

In a large bowl, combine the ground and chopped salmon with soy sauce, mustard, garlic, parsley, egg, and bread crumbs.

Using your hands, shape the salmon into 6 patties, about ½-inch (1 cm) thick. Season with salt.

Heat a skillet over high heat until very hot. If you have an infrared thermometer, the skillet should register at least 500°F (250°C). Or test by brushing on a bit of oil. When the skillet starts to smoke, it is ready.

Brush the skillet with vegetable oil. Place the patties on the skillet without overcrowding. (You may have to do this in batches.) Cook for 3 minutes. Turn the patties over and cook on the other side for 2 minutes until the exterior is crispy and the burgers register an internal temperature of 135°F (57°C).

Transfer the patties to a platter, squeeze with lemon, and tent loosely with foil. While the patties are resting, toast the buns.

To serve: Spread Dill Mayonnaise on the the bottom halves of the buns and place the burgers on top. Add a dollop of crème fraîche, a sprinkle of chives, 2 teaspoons (11 g) of Dilled Salmon Roe (if using), and a few leaves of arugula. Place the remaining halves of buns on top.

Quick and Easy Burger Cookbook

Dill Mayonnaise

1 egg

2 small shallots, diced

1 tablespoon (4 g) minced fresh dill

1 tablespoon (15 ml) fresh lemon juice

2 teaspoons (10 g) Dijon mustard

½ teaspoon (1 g) smoked paprika

1 cup (235 ml) canola or vegetable oil

Kosher salt and fresh cracked black pepper, to taste

—

Yield: 1¾ cups (285 g)

Place the egg, shallots, dill, lemon juice, mustard, and paprika in a food processor or blender and process until smooth.

With the motor running, slowly drizzle in the oil until the mixture is smooth, thick, and shiny, with the consistency of mayonnaise. Season with salt and pepper. Refrigerate for up to 1 week, covered.

Beet Burger

One thing we love about hamburgers is that they always feel like a treat. With veggie burgers, that's often not the case. A lot of times, they can look and taste more like hockey pucks than delicious meals. After a bit of trial and error (we admit it; it wasn't easy), we created a completely vegan burger that has the great meaty texture everyone loves about burgers; and it's delicious. We bet your carnivorous friends will enjoy them as much as those who never touch the animal stuff.

1 large red beet

½ portobello mushroom cap, thickly sliced

Olive oil, for roasting, plus 1 tablespoon (15 ml)

Kosher salt to taste

2 cloves garlic, minced

½ shallot, minced

2 sprigs thyme, stems removed

1 teaspoon (5 ml) soy sauce

1 can (15 ounces, 425 g) white beans, rinsed and drained

2 teaspoons (10 ml) cider vinegar

2 teaspoons (10 g) barbecue dry rub (your favorite brand)

Freshly cracked black pepper, to taste

1 cup (195 g) cooked brown rice, room temperature

Juice from ¾ lemon

½ cup (25 g) panko

2 tablespoons (28 ml) vegetable oil, for cooking

½ zucchini

2 teaspoons (10 ml) olive oil

2 tablespoons (12 g) chopped fresh mint

continued

Preheat the oven to 375°F (190°C, gas mark 5). Wrap the beet in foil and roast until cooked but still firm, about 30 minutes. Cool, peel, and cube (you should have about 1 cup [225 g] cubed beets).

Line a baking sheet with foil. Spread the mushroom slices on the sheet, drizzle with olive oil, and season with salt. Roast for 15 minutes.

In a mixing bowl, toss together the beets, mushroom, garlic, shallot, thyme, and soy sauce. Reserve.

In the bowl of a food processor fitted with the steel blade, process the beans for 20 seconds. Add 1 tablespoon (15 ml) olive oil, vinegar, barbecue rub, salt, and pepper and pulse 3 to 4 times.

Add the beet and mushroom mixture and process for 10 seconds until the beets are incorporated but the mixture is still chunky.

Add the rice and lemon juice and process for 10 more seconds. Transfer to a bowl and fold in the panko.

Shape the mixture into 4 patties, place on a platter, and freeze for ½ hour or refrigerate overnight. Or wrap the burgers individually and freeze for up to 3 months.

Preheat the oven to 325°F (170°C, gas mark 3).

Heat a large cast-iron pan over medium-high heat and add oil.

continued

Beet Burger *(continued)*

4 Flour Bakery Burger Buns
(page 46)

Tomato-Ginger Ketchup
(page 43)

Butter lettuce

—

Yield: 4 burgers

Working with 2 burgers at a time, cook the burgers for 2 minutes per side and then transfer them to an oiled sheet pan. When all the burgers have been cooked, place the sheet pan in the oven for 5 minutes.

While the burgers are baking, thinly slice the zucchini lengthwise, using a mandoline if you have one. Season the zucchini with olive oil and mint.

To serve: Place the burgers on buns, drape 2 pieces of zucchini over the burgers, and garnish with Tomato-Ginger Ketchup and butter lettuce.

Mole-Spiced Turkey Burger

We love deeply flavored mole poblano, with its complex blend of chile peppers, chocolate, cinnamon, and multiple spices, and we wanted to translate the flavors into a burger. Mexico's national dish, the rich, dark sauce is served most often over chicken or turkey. Rather than making a sauce that goes over the burgers, we decided to blend the spices into the meat.

1 six-inch (15 cm) corn tortilla, cut into strips

2 tablespoons (28 ml) chicken or turkey stock, or water

22 ounces (620 g) ground turkey (dark meat)

2 tablespoons (15 g) chili powder

1 tablespoon (5 g) unsweetened cocoa powder

½ teaspoon (1.3 g) cumin seeds, toasted and ground

½ teaspoon (0.9 g) coriander seeds, toasted and ground

2 teaspoons (4.6 g) ground cinnamon

1 green pepper, roasted (see sidebar below) and cut into small dice

2 teaspoons (10 g) kosher salt

Oil for grilling

Kosher salt and fresh cracked black pepper, to taste

4 hamburger buns

Mango Chile Slaw (recipe follows)

In a small bowl, soak the tortilla in the stock or water until soft and then purée in a blender or food processor until smooth.

In a medium bowl, mix the tortilla with the turkey, chili powder, cocoa powder, cumin, coriander, cinnamon, green pepper, and salt until fully incorporated.

Divide the mixture into four 6-ounce (170 g) portions and shape into 4 burgers according to the technique in chapter 1 (see page 13). Refrigerate the burgers, covered, until ready to cook.

Prepare a kettle grill for two-zone grilling (page 16). Clean the grill grate well with a stiff wire brush. Build a hot charcoal fire on one side. Leave the other side empty.

When the fire is hot, brush the grate with oil. Remove the burgers from the refrigerator and season with salt and pepper. Grill directly over the fire for 2 minutes per side. Transfer to the cool side of the grill and cook, covered, for 3 minutes or until a thermometer registers 155°F (68°C). Remove the burgers from the grill and lightly toast the buns.

To serve: Place the burgers on the buns and top with Mango Chile Slaw (see page 88).

—

Yield: 4 burgers

ROASTING PEPPERS

Preheat oven to 450°F (230°C, gas mark 8). Place the peppers on a foil-lined baking sheet, drizzle with a little olive oil and sprinkle with kosher salt. Roast until the peppers are soft and the skins are slightly blackened in spots, 20 to 30 minutes, turning occasionally. Transfer the peppers to a bowl and cover tightly with plastic wrap. Let stand until the peppers are cool enough to handle, about 15 minutes. Remove the skin and seeds from the peppers.

Where's the Beef?

Mango Chile Slaw

4 cups (280 g) green cabbage, shredded, loosely packed (from about ½ head cabbage)

1 red jalapeño pepper, sliced into very thin rings (wear gloves)

¾ cup (27.5 g) slivered almonds, toasted

¾ cup (36 g) peanuts, skin on, toasted and ground

1 teaspoon (2 g) cocoa powder

1 teaspoon (2.3 g) ground cinnamon

1 mango, peeled, seeded, and minced

2 tablespoons (28 ml) olive oil

1 tablespoon (15 ml) fresh lime juice (or more to taste)

1 tablespoon (13 g) sugar

Kosher salt and fresh cracked black pepper, to taste

—

Yield: 4 cups (240 g)

In a large bowl, toss together all ingredients through the sugar. Taste and season with salt and pepper. Cover and refrigerate for up to 3 days.

647's Breakfast Burger

This has been a favorite at Tremont 647's famous Pajama Brunch since the restaurant opened. It will sop up whatever you were imbibing the night before.

647's Breakfast Sausage (recipe follows)

4 slices American cheese

8 slices bacon, cooked to crispy

4 English muffins, toasted

4 eggs, cold from the fridge

Ketchup

—
Yield: 4 burgers

Before you start, have the cheese and hot cooked bacon ready and close at hand.

While the sausage is cooking, put the English muffins in to toast. While the sausage is resting, in a second skillet, cook the eggs to your liking; try to keep them as compact as possible. (Using fresh, cold eggs, straight from the fridge, will help to keep them from spreading out.) If you scramble the eggs, try not to break them up. Instead, fold them, omelet-style, into a square or triangle about the same circumference as your English muffins.

To serve: Place the sausage patties on the muffin bottoms, top with the cheese, bacon, eggs, and ketchup. Top with other halves of muffins. Serve immediately.

647's Breakfast Sausage

There's no way around it. You have to use a grinder for this recipe because it is the best way to get all the flavors to emulsify. The fatback is important as well to keep the sausage juicy.

8 ounces (225 g) pork butt, trimmed and cut into strips

6 ounces (170 g) fatback, rind removed, cut into strips

2 teaspoons (10 g) kosher salt

2 teaspoons (4 g) black pepper, coarsely ground

2 fresh sage leaves, roughly chopped

¾ teaspoon (0.4 g) dried thyme

¾ teaspoon (0.5 g) ground ginger

¾ teaspoon (0.6 g) ground nutmeg

¾ teaspoon (0.3 g) red pepper flakes

1 tablespoon (20 g) maple syrup

3 tablespoons (45 ml) cold water

Vegetable oil, for cooking

—

Yield: 4 patties

Freeze the pork and fatback until stiff but not frozen, about 45 minutes. In a large bowl, toss the meat and spices together. Using the fine grinder disk, grind according to the technique in chapter 1 (see page 13). Mix in the maple syrup and cold water.

Divide the sausage mixture into 4 even portions and shape into patties about 3½ inches (8.5 cm) across.

Heat a skillet over high heat until medium hot. If you have an infrared thermometer, the skillet should register at least 400°F (200°C). Or test by brushing on a bit of oil. When the skillet just barely begins to smoke, it is ready.

Brush oil onto the skillet and cook the patties for 2 minutes on each side. Remove from the skillet and let patties rest for 5 minutes.

FATBACK

Fatback, the fresh layer of fat that runs along the pig's back, is often confused with salt pork (which comes from the sides and belly). A common ingredient in southern cooking, this part of the animal is most often used to make lard and cracklings. Fatback should always be refrigerated. If fresh, it will keep for up to a week. Cured, it can keep for up to a month.

Lamb Juicy Lucy

This is a take on an inside-out cheeseburger, made famous at bars in Minneapolis. The preparation went global, with versions popping up as far away as France. People there stuffed their burgers with Roquefort cheese, instead of the classic American slices used in the Midwest. We imported some Greek influence, stuffing ground lamb with feta cheese and oregano. Extra napkins, please.

3 pounds (1.4 kg) lamb shoulder (or ground lamb)

2 tablespoons (12 g) finely chopped fresh mint

2 tablespoons (8 g) finely chopped fresh parsley

2 tablespoons (28 ml) olive oil

1 tablespoon (6 g) lemon zest

2 cloves garlic, minced

¾ cup (150 g) whole milk Greek yogurt

1 cup (150 g) crumbled feta cheese

6 ounces (170 g) Brie, cut into 6 thin wedges or slices

Kosher salt and fresh cracked black pepper, to taste

Oil, for cooking

2 tablespoons (6 g) dried oregano, preferably Greek

6 eight-inch (20 cm) pita rounds

RECOMMENDED TOPPINGS: Arugula, olive tapenade, thinly sliced cucumber, cherry tomatoes

—
Yield: 6 burgers

Cut the lamb into strips and freeze until stiff but not frozen, about 45 minutes. Grind the lamb according to technique in chapter 1 (see page 13).

In a large bowl, mix the ground lamb with mint, parsley, olive oil, lemon zest, and garlic. Shape into 12 thin patties and set out on a platter or baking sheet.

Spread yogurt on 6 patties, starting from the middle and working out toward the perimeter. Leave about a ½-inch (1 cm) border uncovered all around. Still avoiding the edges, sprinkle feta cheese over the yogurt and top with a piece of Brie. Place the remaining patties on top. Press down firmly with your hands and crimp the edges to seal. Wrap each patty individually in plastic wrap. Refrigerate at least 2 hours or overnight.

These burgers are equally delicious prepared on the grill or skillet. Whichever equipment you use, prepare your cooking surface for high heat. If you're grilling, prepare a kettle grill (see pages 15–16). Clean the grill grate well with a stiff wire brush. Or heat a skillet over high heat until very hot. If you have an infrared thermometer, the skillet should register at least 500°F (250°C). Or test by brushing on a bit of oil. When the skillet starts to smoke, it is ready.

Season the patties with salt and pepper. Brush the grill or skillet with oil. If cooking indoors in a skillet, cook for 3 to 5 minutes per side until a thermometer inserted into a burger registers 125°F (52°C). If grilling, cook for 3 to 5 minutes per side. Transfer the burgers to a platter, sprinkle with oregano, and allow to rest for 3 minutes.

To serve: Slit pita rounds open and place 1 burger inside each. Spread with tapenade and top with arugula, cucumbers, and/or tomatoes.

Jesse's Bison Burger

Having owned a restaurant for 16 years, Andy has had the opportunity to work with a lot of talented chefs. Jesse Ford-Diamond is one of the most notable. When he heard we were writing a burger book, he told us we had to try his. And he was right. Not only is this burger über-tasty, it's a great use of ground bison (often referred to and sold as buffalo), which has justifiably been gaining popularity because of its excellent flavor and leanness.

SALAD

1 large or 2 small local heirloom tomatoes, cored and sliced

½ small red onion, julienned

1 roasted red pepper, peeled, seeded, and julienned

1 tablespoon (15 ml) balsamic vinegar

1 tablespoon (15 ml) olive oil

1 tablespoon (4 g) minced fresh Italian flat-leaf parsley leaves

6 basil leaves, julienned

1 clove garlic, minced

Kosher salt and fresh cracked black pepper, to taste

BURGERS

1½ pounds (680 g) ground bison, 90 percent lean

½ teaspoon (2.5 g) kosher salt

1 teaspoon (2 g) fresh cracked black pepper

8 ounces (225 g) fresh mozzarella, cut into 8 slices

4 whole wheat burger buns

2 ounces (55 g) baby arugula

Red Wine–Basil Aioli (recipe follows)

—

Yield: 4 burgers

In a medium bowl, mix together the tomatoes, red onion, roasted red pepper, vinegar, olive oil, parsley, basil, and garlic. Season with salt and pepper to taste. Cover and reserve until burgers are ready.

Prepare a two-zone fire according to the instructions in chapter 1 (page 16).

While the coals are heating, in a separate bowl, combine the ground bison with salt and cracked pepper and mix well. Shape into 4 burgers according to the technique in chapter 1 (page 13).

Place the burgers on the grill grate directly over the coals and sear for 2 minutes on each side. Move the burgers to the cool side of the grill, top each one with 2 slices of mozzarella, and cover the grill. Cook for 3 minutes or until the cheese is melted.

To serve: Spread Red Wine–Basil Aioli on bottom halves of buns, place burgers on buns, top with Marinated Vegetable Salad and a few leaves of arugula, and lay the top halves of the buns on the salad. Serve immediately.

Red Wine-Basil Aioli

1 large egg

2 cloves garlic, peeled

6 basil leaves, chopped

2 teaspoons (10 ml) red wine vinegar

½ cup (120 ml) olive oil

½ cup (120 ml) canola oil

Kosher salt and fresh cracked black pepper, to taste

—

Yield: 1¾ cups (285 g)

Place the egg, garlic, basil, and red wine vinegar in the bowl of a food processor or blender and process until smooth.

Mix the two oils in a small bowl. With the motor running, slowly drizzle the oil into the food processor until the mixture is smooth, thick, and shiny, with the consistency of mayonnaise. Season with salt and pepper. Refrigerate for up to 1 week, covered.

CHAPTER 5

Burgers Beyond Borders

In the early 1970s, when McDonald's opened its first non-American stores in Japan, Holland, Australia, Germany, and France, the American hamburger went global. More recently, highly pedigreed chefs from around the world started creating their own versions of haute burgers on our shores, incorporating ingredients like foie gras, truffles, and Kobe beef. The humble burger wasn't always so humble anymore.

We highly support the idea of the global burger. But we take a slightly different approach. In our years of international travel, we have come to love certain flavors, like fiery Asian chiles, tropical spice blends, and minty Greek yogurt sauce, and incorporate them into our food whenever we can. In this chapter, we have burgers that grew out of our worldly adventures. Like our Bulgogi Burger. We knew the flavors of Korean bulgogi, one of our favorite beef dishes, would translate to burgers, and we were right. When Andrea's son, Luke, made us Chickpea Burgers after returning from a stay in Morocco, using ingredients he bought in the Marrakech spice souk, we were so taken with the patties that we knew we had to include them here.

Banh Mi Burger

These oblong-shaped patties, served on baguettes instead of traditional hamburger rolls, are a takeoff on Vietnamese banh mi sandwiches. A culinary legacy of France's colonial rule in Vietnam, the sandwiches draw from both cultures, as does our burger—with a nod to our northern neighbors, French Canada.

We use the reverse-sear method for these burgers, which allows the meat to cook through yet stay juicy inside. At the last minute, just before serving, we transfer it to the stovetop and create a nice crust in the skillet. The Pork Corton should be made the day before you plan to serve these.

2½ pounds (1.1 kg) boneless pork shoulder or butt

3 tablespoons (45 ml) fish sauce (preferably Red Boat brand)

1 tablespoon (6 g) minced fresh ginger

2 teaspoons (10 g) palm sugar or light brown sugar

2 teaspoons (9 g) Chinese chili garlic sauce

1 clove garlic, minced

1 teaspoon (5 ml) soy sauce

1 teaspoon (2 g) fresh cracked white pepper

½ teaspoon (2.5 ml) sesame oil

½ cup (25 g) panko

Peanut oil, for cooking

Lime wedge

2 baguettes, hollowed out and cut into thirds

1 cup (225 g) mayonnaise (we prefer Kewpie mayonnaise, found in many Asian markets)

Pork Corton (recipe follows)

½ English cucumber, thinly sliced

1 carrot, shredded

½ jalapeño pepper, thinly sliced

continued

Freeze the pork until stiff but not frozen, about 1 hour.

Using the coarse grinder plate, grind the pork according to the technique in chapter 1 (see page 13). Refrigerate until ready to use.

Line a sheet pan with parchment paper. Preheat the oven to 275°F (140°C, gas mark 1).

In a large bowl, combine the ground pork, fish sauce, ginger, brown sugar, chili sauce, garlic, soy sauce, white pepper, and sesame oil. Carefully fold in the bread crumbs.

With moistened hands, shape the mixture into 6 flat, oval patties, about ¾ inch (2 cm) thick.

Place the patties on the parchment-lined pans and bake on the center rack of the oven for 30 minutes or until an instant-read thermometer registers 145°F (63°C).

Remove from the oven and heat a skillet over high heat until very hot. If you have an infrared thermometer, the skillet should register at least 500°F (250°C). Or test by brushing on a bit of oil. When the skillet starts to smoke, it is ready.

Brush the peanut oil onto the skillet and sear the patties for 1 minute. Using a thin, flexible metal spatula, carefully turn the patties over and sear the other side for 1 minute.

Remove the burgers to the sheet pan, squeeze them with the lime wedge, and let the burgers rest while you toast the baguettes.

continued

Quick and Easy Burger Cookbook

Banh Mi Burger *(continued)*

Cilantro, mint, and basil leaves

6 pieces butter lettuce

SPECIAL EQUIPMENT:
Grinder attachment to stand mixer, parchment paper

—

Yield: 6 burgers

Wipe out the griddle. Spread the cut sides of the baguettes with the mayonnaise and place on the griddle over very low heat until the mayonnaise starts to brown, just about a minute. Transfer to a platter, toasted side up.

Assemble the burgers: Place a burger on the bottom half of each roll. Smear a generous amount of Pork Corton on the top halves of the baguettes. Layer the cucumber, carrot, jalapeño, herbs, and butter lettuce on the burgers. Place the top halves of the baguettes on the burgers and serve immediately.

Pork Corton

This pork spread, a Quebecois staple (also known as cretons in French-speaking Canada), is similar to rillettes or pork pâté. Geographical proximity has made the dish fairly common in parts of northern New England as well. We learned to make it after spending some time in Montreal. It is perfect for spreading on toast or our Banh Mi Burger (page 98).

2 pounds (900 g) pork shoulder, including as much fat as possible, cut in pieces to fit in grinder tube

1 cup (235 ml) milk

1 medium onion, minced

1 tablespoon (15 ml) Maggi Seasoning (see Resources, page 138)

1 tablespoon (15 g) kosher salt

½ cup (60 g) fine dry bread crumbs

SPECIAL EQUIPMENT: Grinder attachment to stand mixer

—

Yield: 5 cups

Freeze the pork shoulder until stiff but not frozen, about 1 hour.

Grind the pork and pork fat using the coarse grinder plate and then grind it again using the fine grinder plate.

In a large saucepan over medium-low heat, cook the ground meat, milk, onion, Maggi Seasoning, and salt until it begins to simmer, stirring and folding to blend the milk into the pork. Reduce the heat to low and cook for 1½ hours, stirring occasionally. Add the bread crumbs and cook for another ½ hour.

Remove from the heat and cool to room temperature.

The fat will have separated during cooling. Fold the fat into the pork mixture and spoon the corton into a crock or bowl. Cover tightly with plastic wrap and refrigerate overnight.

Moroccan Chickpea Burger

When Andrea's son, Luke, lived in Morocco, he made a couple of trips to Fez, a city known for its beauty, culture, and history. While there, he always made sure to stop at Café Clock, a popular spot owned and operated by a colorful British ex-pat. He couldn't get enough of the famed camel burger, but the café also boasts a wonderful chickpea burger, flavored with preserved lemons, a local staple. Luke's adaptation follows.

2 (19-ounce, 535 g) cans chickpeas, drained and rinsed

3 cloves garlic, peeled and mashed

Rind of 1 preserved lemon, chopped

1 egg

1½ teaspoons (4 g) cumin powder

1 teaspoon (2 g) ground coriander

¾ teaspoon (0.5 g) ground ginger

Handful fresh parsley leaves

Kosher salt and ground white pepper, to taste

1 red onion, roughly chopped

3 tablespoons (17 g) chickpea flour

Oil, for cooking (1 to 2 tablespoons (15 to 28 ml)

6 egg rolls, split in half horizontally

Harissa Mayo (recipe follows)

Parsley Salad (recipe follows)

—
Yield: 6 burgers

In the bowl of a food processor fitted with the steel blade, combine the chickpeas, garlic, preserved lemon rind, egg, cumin powder, coriander, ginger, parsley, salt, and white pepper. Pulse 6 to 7 times. Transfer two-thirds of the mixture to a bowl and process the remaining mixture until smooth. Fold the chickpea purée into the chunkier mixture and then fold in the chopped onion and chickpea flour. Using a large spoon or ice cream scoop, divide the mixture into 6 even portions and shape into patties.

Pour enough oil into a large skillet to coat the bottom. Set over medium-high heat and cook patties for 3 to 4 minutes until golden brown. Flip the patties and cook the other side for 3 to 4 minutes until golden. Transfer to a plate.

Turn the heat to low and place the rolls, cut sides down, in the skillet. Heat for just under a minute until lightly brown. (You may have to do this in batches.)

To serve: Slather the tops and bottoms of the rolls with Harissa Mayo and place burgers on bottoms of rolls. Mound on some Parsley Salad and top with the other half of the bun.

Burgers Beyond Borders

Harissa Mayo

½ cup (115 g) Best.Mayo.Ever.
(page 23) or your favorite
mayonnaise

⅓ cup (85 g) harissa (North
African chile paste; available at
most Middle Eastern markets,
or see Resources, page 138)

—

Yield: Scant ¾ cup (200 g)

In a small bowl, stir the mayo and harissa together.
Refrigerate, covered, until needed or up to 1 week.

Parsley Salad

1 small bunch fresh parsley
leaves, roughly chopped

2 teaspoons (10 ml) fresh
lemon juice or to taste

1 teaspoon (5 ml) olive oil

Coarse sea salt to taste

—

**Yield: 6 servings
as burger topping**

In a medium bowl, mix together the parsley, lemon juice,
and olive oil with your hands. Sprinkle with sea salt.

Gold Coast Burger

When we travel internationally, we are always fascinated to see how American food has influenced the local cuisine. Making his way along Australia's Gold Coast, Chris happened on this wild rendition of our nation's culinary icon. It's usually made with kangaroo meat Down Under. We didn't think that would go over too well back home, so we adapted it a bit. The beets, pineapple, bacon, and fried egg are true to the original. Cook these on your barbie, mate.

1½ pounds (680 g) freshly ground chuck

Kosher salt and fresh cracked black pepper, to taste

1 tablespoon (7 g) Fifth Dimension Powder (page 25)

½ cup (58 g) shredded sharp Cheddar cheese

Aussie Special Sauce (recipe follows)

Caramelized Onions (recipe follows)

4 slices canned pickled beets, drained

4 slices tomato, thinly sliced and seasoned with cracked pepper

1 cup (72 g) shredded iceberg lettuce

Oil, for frying

4 slices Canadian bacon

4 slices canned pineapple rings, patted dry

4 eggs

4 hamburger buns

—
Yield: 4 burgers

Prepare a kettle grill (see pages 15–16). Clean the grill grate well with a stiff wire brush. While the grill is heating, form the patties. Divide the meat into 4 equal portions and shape according to the technique in chapter 1 (see page 13).

When the fire is hot (you can hold your hands over it for 5 seconds), brush the grill grates with oil. Season the burgers with salt and pepper and place on the grill grates. Grill for 4 minutes and flip. Grill 3 minutes longer or until medium rare (130°F [54°C] internal temperature). Transfer the burgers to a platter. Sprinkle with Fifth Dimension Powder and Cheddar cheese. Tent with foil and let rest for 10 minutes.

Prepare the condiment platter: Arrange Aussie Special Sauce, Caramelized Onions, drained pickled beets, sliced tomatoes, and shredded lettuce on a platter.

In a large sauté pan over medium-high heat, fry the Canadian bacon in tablespoon (15 ml) of oil for 2 to 3 minutes until crispy. Turn the bacon over and fry for another 2 to 3 minutes until the other side is crispy. Blot with paper towels and transfer to the platter with the beets, tomatoes, and lettuce.

In the same pan over medium heat, sauté the pineapple slices in the leftover bacon fat until just brown, about 2 minutes per side. Transfer to the platter.

Crack the eggs into the same pan. Turn the heat to medium. Cover and cook for 5 minutes. Do not turn them over (you want them sunny-side up). Season with salt and set on platter.

Assemble the burger: Spread Aussie Special Sauce on the top and bottom of each bun. Sprinkle the shredded lettuce over the bottoms. Place the burgers on the the lettuce. Layer on the onions, Canadian bacon, pineapple, beet, tomato, and egg. Place the tops on and enjoy.

Aussie Special Sauce

¾ cup (60 g) Kewpie mayonnaise (see Resources, page 138)

¾ cup (70 g) chili garlic sauce (preferably Vietnamese)

—

Yield: ½ cup (115 g)

In a small bowl, stir the mayonnaise and chili garlic sauce together. Refrigerate until ready to use.

Caramelized Onions

1 tablespoon (15 ml) olive oil

2 large sweet onions, peeled and sliced

1 teaspoon (6 g) salt

1 tablespoon (15 ml) water

—

Yield: 1 cup (150 g)

Heat the olive oil in a large, nonstick sauté pan over medium-high heat. Add the onions and salt and cook, stirring often, until the onions soften and just start to brown. Reduce the heat to medium low and cook, stirring occasionally, until the onions collapse completely and turn to a rich, jammy brown, about 30 minutes. When the onions are nearly done, add 1 tablespoon (15 ml) water and stir, scraping the browned bits from the bottom of the pan into the onions. Set aside to cool.

Bulgogi Burger

We love the combination of flavors in this Korean dish. Cornstarch helps the burger get a gorgeous crust, and the soy caramelizes nicely around it.

BURGERS

1½ pounds (680 g) chuck or ground beef

1 tablespoon (6 g) peeled and minced fresh ginger

2 cloves garlic, minced

2 tablespoons (28 ml) soy sauce

2 teaspoons (10 ml) sesame oil

2 scallions, cut into ⅛-inch (3 mm) rings, whites and greens

½ cup (64 g) cornstarch, for dusting

Vegetable oil, for cooking

SAUCE

¾ cup (60 ml) soy sauce

2 tablespoons (40 g) agave nectar or honey

1 tablespoon (16 g) chili garlic paste or sambal

1 tablespoon (15 ml) sesame oil

1 tablespoon (15 g) packed brown sugar

2 teaspoons (5 g) white sesame seeds, toasted

2 teaspoons (5 g) black sesame seeds

1 teaspoon (2 g) peeled and minced fresh ginger

1 large clove garlic, minced

1 teaspoon (2 g) fresh cracked white pepper

4 hamburger buns, toasted

Sesame Aioli (recipe follows)

Quick Kimchi (recipe follows)

—

Yield: 4 burgers

Make the burgers: If you are grinding, in a large bowl combine the chuck, ginger, garlic, soy sauce, and sesame oil. Marinate, refrigerated, for 30 minutes to 1 hour, tossing every 10 minutes. Grind according to the technique in chapter 1 (page 13) and then fold in the scallions. Shape into 4 burgers according to the technique in chapter 1 (page 13).

For ground beef, mix the beef with all ingredients through scallions and then follow the shaping technique in chapter 1 (page 13) to make 4 burgers.

Spread the cornstarch on a plate. Lay the burger down to coat on one side and then turn over to coat the other side. Tap to remove the excess and transfer to another plate in a single layer. Repeat with the remaining burgers.

Make the sauce: In a small bowl, combine the soy sauce and the following nine ingredients and mix well.

Heat a skillet over high heat until very hot. The skillet should register at least 500°F (250°C). Or test by brushing on a bit of oil. When the skillet starts to smoke, it is ready.

Oil the skillet and sear the burgers for 2 minutes, flipping the burgers and searing the second side for 2 minutes. Reduce the heat to medium, stir the sauce, and spoon over the burgers. Cook for 1 minute, remove the burgers, and let rest.

To serve: Spread Sesame Aioli (recipe follows) on buns. Serve with Quick Kimchi, either on top of burgers or on the side.

Quick Kimchi

Disclaimer: We are huge fans of kimchi. Traditionally, this spicy Korean condiment ferments for days—or longer—in a cool, dark place. Here is a quick version that is very, very tasty. But nobody would accuse it of being traditional.

½ small head Napa cabbage, cored and cut into 1-inch (2.5 cm) cubes

1 cucumber, peeled, sliced into ¾-inch (6 mm) thick slices

1 red onion, julienned

1 tablespoon (16 g) chili garlic paste, sambal, or Sriracha

2 teaspoons (4 g) peeled and minced fresh ginger

1 teaspoon (5 g) kosher salt

—

Yield: About 12 cups (720 g)

Mix all ingredients in a bowl, cover tightly with plastic wrap, and let sit out for 4 hours. Mix again. Refrigerate until needed and up to 1 week.

Sesame Aioli

1 egg

1 tablespoon (15 ml) fresh lime juice, plus zest from lime, minced

1 tablespoon (6 g) peeled and minced fresh ginger

1 tablespoon (16 g) chili garlic paste or sambal

1 cup (235 ml) canola oil

1 tablespoon (15 ml) sesame oil

1 tablespoon (15 ml) soy sauce

Fresh cracked black pepper, to taste

—

Yield: 1¾ cups (285 g)

Place the egg, lime juice, ginger, and chili garlic paster or sambal in a food processor. Process until smooth.

Mix the two oils in a small bowl. With the motor running, slowly drizzle oil into the food processor until the mixture is smooth, thick, and shiny, with the consistency of mayonnaise. Add the soy sauce and season with pepper. Refrigerate for up to 1 week, covered.

Gyro Burger

Traditionally, a gyro is a Greek specialty of meat—usually lamb—roasted on a vertical spit, often wrapped in soft pita bread with onions, tomatoes, and tzatziki sauce. Perfect street food, the gyro is made for food trucks. But we're taking it in another direction. Instead of roasting the meat on a spit, we're adding the spices usually associated with the roasted meat to ground lamb and shaping it into patties. Welcome to the Gyro Burger. Take it on the road or enjoy it at home with friends.

1½ pounds (680 g) ground lamb

2 tablespoons (28 ml) olive oil, plus more for cooking

1 tablespoon (7 g) smoked or sweet paprika

1 teaspoon (1 g) dried oregano

Kosher salt to taste

4 large rounds pita bread

Tzatziki Sauce (recipe follows)

1 medium red onion, thinly sliced

1 medium tomato, seeded and chopped, seasoned with black pepper

1 clove garlic, minced

1 tablespoon (6 g) chopped fresh mint

1 batch Wicked Good Fries (page 116)

—
Yield: 4 burgers

In a large bowl, combine the lamb with the olive oil, paprika, and oregano. Divide into 4 equal portions and shape into oval patties that are ¾-inch (2 cm) thick. Season both sides with salt.

Heat a skillet over high heat until very hot. If you have an infrared thermometer, the skillet should register at least 500°F (250°C). Or test by brushing on a bit of oil. When the skillet starts to smoke, it is ready.

Brush oil onto the skillet and cook the burgers for 3 minutes per side or until internal temperature reaches 135°F (57°C). Transfer the burgers to a platter to rest for 5 minutes.

Brush the pita rounds with olive oil and toast both sides on the griddle until lightly brown and soft.

Spread ¾ cup Tzatziki Sauce (65 g) on the bottom of each pita. Place burger on top of sauce. Garnish with onion, tomato, and fries and spread a bit more Tzatziki Sauce on top of the fries. Sprinkle with garlic and mint. Roll the pita around each burger and seal tight with a piece of butcher paper or aluminum foil.

Tzatziki Sauce

1 cup (200 g) plain Greek yogurt

1 tablespoon (8 g) minced, seeded cucumber

1 tablespoon (6 g) minced fresh mint

1 clove garlic, minced

2 teaspoons (10 ml) extra-virgin olive oil

½ teaspoon (2.5 g) kosher salt

Juice of ¾ lemon

—
Yield 1¾ cups (300 g)

Place the yogurt in a fine strainer set over a mixing bowl and refrigerate for 2 hours.

Transfer the strained yogurt to a bowl and stir in remaining ingredients. Refrigerate until ready to use.

Herb Salad

1 cucumber, peeled and cut into ⅛-inch (3 mm) discs

½ red onion, peeled, cored, and cut as thin as possible

20 cilantro leaves

8 basil leaves, roughly chopped

8 mint leaves, roughly chopped

DRESSING
2 tablespoons (28 ml) fish sauce

1 tablespoon (15 ml) fresh lime juice

1 tablespoon (20 g) agave nectar or honey

—

Yield: 6 servings

For salad: Place the salad ingredients in a bowl and toss lightly.

For dressing: In a small bowl, mix well. Refrigerate until ready to use.

About 10 minutes before serving, toss the salad with the dressing. (For scallop burgers, dress salad just before frying burgers.)

Spiced Aioli

1 egg

1 shallot, peeled and roughly chopped

20 cilantro leaves

2 tablespoons (28 ml) fresh lime juice

1 tablespoon (16 g) chili garlic paste or sambal

2 teaspoons (10 g) Dijon mustard

1 cup (235 ml) canola oil

1 tablespoon (15 ml) sesame oil

1 tablespoon (15 ml) soy sauce

Kosher salt and fresh cracked black pepper, to taste

—

Yield: 1¾ cups (405 g)

Place the egg, shallot, cilantro, lime juice, chili garlic paste or sambal, and mustard in a food processor or blender. Process until smooth.

Mix the two oils in a small bowl. With the motor running, slowly drizzle into the food processor until the mixture is smooth, thick, and shiny, with the consistency of mayonnaise. Add the soy sauce and season with salt and pepper. Refrigerate for up to 1 week, covered.

Burgers Beyond Borders

CHAPTER 6

You Want Fries with That?

It's an automatic question. Order a burger, and the server asks, "You want fries with that?" And the answer, almost unfailingly, is "Yes!" Burgers and fries are such a classic combination that we felt we had to dedicate a chapter to fried, crunchy things to eat with your burgers. So this chapter includes not only a variety of fries—one of which, Sweet Potato Pub Fries, is actually baked, not fried—but potato chips and onion rings as well.

Our perfectly crispy french fry is actually a twice-cooked fry. We elaborate on the technique in our Wicked Good Fries recipe, in which the potatoes are first slow-cooked in oil at low heat, cooled, and then fried. It's the way most restaurants do it and it's very doable for home cooks, too.

Wicked Good Fries

It is generally believed that the french fry, our national vegetable, originated in Belgium, which is also the country with the highest per capita consumption of this irresistible indulgence. In terms of overall consumption, however, nobody can beat the good old U.S. of A.

The preparation method below is similar to one used for duck confit because first you cook the potatoes at low heat and then fry them at high heat. In a restaurant, it's how we make them crispy yet extremely tender. Some people call these confit fries. As far as we're concerned, this is the best way to make french fries as good as any burger joint's.

4 baker or Russet potatoes, about ½ pound (225 g) each, washed

Oil for frying

Kosher salt and fresh cracked black pepper for seasoning, or your favorite seasoning

SPECIAL EQUIPMENT: Deep fryer, vegetable/french fry cutter (see Resources, page 138)

—

Yield: 4 to 6 servings

Preheat fryer to 275°F (140°C).

Cut the potatoes lengthwise into ¾-inch (6 mm) wide fries. Place in a deep bowl or bucket and rinse with cold water until clear to remove all excess starch. Pour the contents of the bowl into a colander placed in the sink. Leave the potatoes in the colander, giving it a light toss to try to remove as much water as possible.

Fill the fryer basket no more than half full with potatoes and place in the preheated oil. The potatoes will cook slowly, barely bubbling. Cook for 3 to 5 minutes until the fries are al dente. To test, reach in with tongs and carefully remove one fry. It should snap easily between two fingers but not be mushy. Spread the fries in a single layer on a drying rack on a sheet pan, cool to room temperature, and then refrigerate until cold, 45 minutes to an hour. Store, sealed in an airtight container, for up to 4 days.

When you are ready to serve: Preheat the deep fryer to 350°F (180°C).

Fill the basket half full with the fries and drop into preheated oil. Fry for 3 to 6 minutes until golden brown and crisp. Place on a drying towel or paper bag and season with salt and pepper or your favorite seasoning. Serve immediately.

Quick and Easy Burger Cookbook

Feed potato into French fry cutter.

Apply light pressure.

Perfect form

Wicked good frying

Quick and Easy Burger Cookbook

Creole Fries

Andy serves many orders of these nightly at his restaurant, Tremont 647. They are a perfect match with the Rosemary Aioli. Toss Wicked Good Fries with a generous helping of Creole Seasoning (it works best when the fries are still really hot) and serve with a side of Rosemary Aioli for dipping.

CREOLE SEASONING
2 tablespoons (5.4 g) dried thyme

2 tablespoons (4 g) dried basil

2 tablespoons (7 g) paprika

1 tablespoon (6.3 g) gumbo filé powder

1 tablespoon (5.3 g) cayenne pepper

1 teaspoon (2.6 g) chili powder

1 bay leaf, ground or finely chopped

—

Yield: Approximately ½ cup (32 g)

Combine all the ingredients in a small bowl and mix thoroughly. The rub will stay fresh for up to 3 months, stored in an airtight container in a cool, dark place.

Rosemary Aioli

1 egg

1 tablespoon (15 ml) fresh lemon juice

2 cloves garlic, peeled and chopped

1 tablespoon (1.7 g) minced fresh rosemary leaves

2 teaspoons (10 g) Dijon mustard

1 cup (235 ml) canola oil

Kosher salt and fresh cracked black pepper, to taste

—

Yield: 1¾ cups (280 g)

Place the egg, lemon juice, garlic, rosemary, and mustard in a food processor or blender. Process until smooth.

With the motor running, slowly drizzle the oil into the food processor until the mixture is smooth, thick, and shiny, with the consistency of mayonnaise. Season with salt and pepper. Refrigerate for up to 1 week, covered.

Duck Fat Fries

We've had duck fat fries and beef fat fries at many restaurants, and they are always tremendous. The flavors from the fats are rich and decadent, and the fries are so easy to make at home that we're giving you two options. The first is to follow the recipe for Wicked Good Fries on page 116 and substitute the fry oil with duck fat or beef fat. You can buy it from your local butcher. They may have to order it, so plan ahead.

The second, below, is a twist that doesn't require you to buy a lot of duck fat and will blow people away. We recognize that you can't just go to your supermarket to buy duck skin. If you don't have any hanging around the house (and you might—we know some of you cook duck breasts), you can substitute bacon in the seasoning.

DUCK FAT FRIES SEASONING
Skin of 4 duck breasts
(or 8 slices bacon)

1 tablespoon (15 g) coarse
sea salt, such as Maldon

¾ cup (9.6 g) fresh
thyme leaves

DUCK FAT VINAIGRETTE
¾ cup (15 g) fresh flat-leaf
Italian parsley, roughly
chopped

2 tablespoons (28 ml)
fresh lemon juice

1 tablespoon (15 g)
Dijon mustard

1 tablespoon (15 ml)
extra-virgin olive oil

1 teaspoon (1.8 g)
togarashi pepper

¾ cup (55 g) reserved duck fat,
room temperature

Kosher salt and fresh cracked
black pepper, to taste

—
Yield: 4 to 6 servings

DUCK FAT FRIES SEASONING

Set a metal cooling rack in a sheet pan lined with foil. Preheat oven to 275°F (140°C, gas mark 1).

Spray the cooling rack with cooking spray. Lay the duck skin flat on the cooling rack. Place in the preheated oven and cook for about 1½ to 2 hours until golden brown and crispy. Remove from the oven and let cool. Reserve the fat from the pan and save ¾ cup (55 g) for Duck Fat Vinaigrette. Do not refrigerate. (If using bacon, cook on the stovetop until very crisp. Transfer the bacon to a paper towel–lined plate to cool. Reserve the fat for the vinaigrette.)

Once the skin is cool, chop until there are no pieces bigger than ¾ inch (6 mm). Place in a small bowl and using your hands, mix well with the sea salt and fresh thyme, breaking up any large pieces of salt. Set aside until you are ready to season the fries.

DUCK FAT VINAIGRETTE

In a small bowl, combine the parsley, lemon juice, mustard, olive oil, togarashi pepper, and reserved duck fat. Mix well and season with kosher salt and fresh cracked black pepper. Set aside.

WICKED GOOD FRIES (PAGE 116)
Make the fries.

To serve: Place the fries in a bowl or on a large platter, drizzle with Duck Fat Vinaigrette, and then sprinkle Duck Fat Fries Seasoning over it.

Sweet Potato Pub Fries

We love the rich creaminess of sweet potatoes. Though this recipe does not involve any frying, the potatoes are crispy and delicious. To take them over the top, apply the Sweet Potato Dust right after they come out of the oven. They are also fantastic with Tomato-Ginger Ketchup.

2 large sweet potatoes, washed, unpeeled, each cut into 8 wedges

1 tablespoon (15 ml) olive oil, plus more for baking sheet

Kosher salt and fresh cracked black pepper, to taste

—

Yield: 6 servings

Preheat oven to 425°F (220°C, gas mark 7).

In a large bowl, toss the sweet potatoes with the olive oil and season with salt and pepper. Place on an oiled baking sheet, with a cut side down. Bake for 10 minutes, turn the wedges over, and bake for another 10 minutes until the potatoes are golden to dark golden brown (depending on how crunchy you like them). Season with salt and pepper or Sweet Potato Dust. Serve immediately with Tomato-Ginger Ketchup (page 43).

Sweet Potato Dust

1 teaspoon (2 g) fennel seeds, toasted and ground

1 teaspoon (1.8 g) coriander seeds, toasted and ground

½ teaspoon (0.6 g) crushed red pepper flakes

2 teaspoons (10 g) sea salt

½ teaspoon (1 g) ground white pepper

2 teaspoons (10 g) packed brown sugar

In a small bowl, mix all ingredients together. Store, covered, in a cool, dry place for up to 1 month.

—

Yield: About ½ cup (32 g), or enough for 4 batches of fries

FROM POTATOES TO FRIES

In the restaurant, it's easy to turn potatoes into fries. We have equipment that helps us cut a 50-pound (22.7 kg) case into beautiful, uniformly shaped fries in about 15 minutes. We're guessing you don't have one at home. there is a pretty good plastic vegetable/french fry cutter you can buy for less than 20 dollars (see Resources, page 138). A mandoline works well, too.

The Idaho Potato Commission tells us the three most common sizes for fries are, in order of popularity: ¾-inch (6 mm) shoestring, ⅜-inch (9 mm) straight cut, and 5/16-inch (8 mm) straight cut.

Our favorite is the ¾-inch (6 mm), which is what we recommend in our recipes. You can peel them, but we prefer more rustic fries with the skins on.

Wicked Good Poutine

We can think of no better way to take down three days' worth of calories in under 10 minutes than with a heaping platter of poutine. We don't recommend a steady diet of it, but sometimes you can't beat this salty, crunchy, tangy, greasy, delicious mess—which also happens to go really well with burgers. The classic version calls for cheese curds, but we find that sharp provolone gives it a nice kick.

Wicked Good Fries (page 116)

4 tablespoons (½ stick, 55 g) butter

4 tablespoons (31 g) flour

2¾ cups (535 ml) beef stock or highest-quality canned beef broth

Kosher salt and fresh cracked black pepper, to taste

6 ounces (170 g) sharp provolone, cut into medium dice

2 tablespoons (6 g) minced chives

—
Yield: 4 to 6 servings

Prepare the fries through the low-temperature cooking and refrigerate.

While the fries are chilling, make the gravy: In a large saucepan over medium heat, melt the butter. Whisk in the flour. Cook gently, whisking often, until the mixture turns a dark, caramelly brown, about 10 minutes. Watch carefully, adjusting the heat if necessary and scraping the bottom of the pan so the mixture darkens evenly and does not burn. Add the stock and simmer, stirring often, 15 minutes or until mixture is smooth and thickened to gravy. Taste and season with salt and pepper and keep warm.

Cook the fries for a second time according to instructions on page 116. Arrange on a platter and scatter provolone evenly over the fries. Ladle a generous portion of hot gravy over the pile and sprinkle with chives. Loosen your belt and dig in.

Green Krack Sauce

We crave this sauce. We dream about this sauce. Chefs Seth and Angela serve it with ceviche and oysters. We think it's great with anything, especially these onion rings. Though Seth and Angela have never shared the recipe with us, we did our best to re-create their incredible sauce, so unless you are on Nantucket, this will have to do.

2 cloves garlic, peeled

½ cup (8 g) finely chopped cilantro leaves

2 tablespoons (28 ml) yuzu juice

2 tablespoons (28 ml) fresh lime juice

2 tablespoons (28 ml) fish sauce

3 tablespoons (60 g) agave nectar or honey

1 tablespoon (3 g) minced chives

1 teaspoon (1.2 g) red pepper flakes

—

Yield: About 1 cup (175 g)

With the motor running, drop the garlic through the lid of a blender and purée. Stop the motor and add the remaining ingredients. Purée until smooth. Use within a few hours.

CHAPTER 7

That's a Frappe!

When we think of the golden age of the burger, we envision the classic malt shop—think American Graffiti *or* Happy Days—*the kind of place serving burgers, fries, and shakes that is practically extinct. But you can re-create the experience yourself, argyle sweaters and bobby socks optional.*

First, a word about shakes. In most of the United States, a milkshake is a thick, delicious drink made from milk, syrup, and ice cream blended together. But we're from Boston, and where we come from that same delicious drink is called a frappe. We don't know why. It just is. And it's wicked good.

In this chapter, we offer frappes in traditional flavors that recall the golden age—you can't really improve on chocolate and vanilla—and a couple of newer flavor combinations we've come to love, like Salted Caramel. Our root beer float is pretty classic, with homemade vanilla ice cream. But you might not have tried anything like our Ginger Beer Float with homemade Coconut Ice Cream. We also recommend some alcohol pairings to make your frappes and floats Wicked.

And just for fun, we offer a dessert burger, with its own Brioche Bun.

Vanilla Frappe

When we were young and foolish, we scorned anything vanilla, being drawn instead to the sexier, more alluring chocolate. Happily, we have come to appreciate that there is nothing "plain" about this aromatic spice—particularly when it is the primary flavor in a thick, smooth frappe.

6 ounces (175 ml) very cold milk

½ vanilla bean

½ teaspoon (2.5 ml) pure vanilla extract

4 generous scoops Vanilla Ice Cream (about 1 ½ cups [210 g], recipe follows, or your favorite premium brand)

MAKE IT WICKED: add 1 ounce (28 ml) of your favorite single-malt scotch after the vanilla extract.

—

Yield: One 16-ounce (475 ml) or two 8-ounce (235 ml) frappes

Pour the milk into the container of a blender or drink mixer. Slice open the vanilla bean and scrape the seeds into the milk. Add the vanilla extract, followed by the ice cream. Using the blender's purée setting, blend for 45 seconds to 1 minute until the mixture is thick and smooth. (If using a mixer, start on the slow speed and accelerate after a few seconds.)

Vanilla Ice Cream

2 cups (475 ml) cream

1 cup (235 ml) whole milk

1 vanilla bean, split

6 egg yolks

¾ cup (150 g) sugar

SPECIAL EQUIPMENT:
Ice cream maker

—

Yield: About 1 quart (1 L)

In a heavy-bottomed saucepan over medium heat, combine the cream, milk, and vanilla bean. Heat until small bubbles start to form around the edges of the pan. Remove from the heat and set aside.

In a medium bowl, beat the egg yolks and sugar together by hand with a whisk until they are thick and light.

Gradually add about half of the hot cream and milk mixture, whisking until smooth. Pour the contents of the bowl back into the saucepan and mix well.

Place the pan over medium-low heat and cook, stirring constantly, until the mixture thickens enough to coat the back of a spoon and registers just barely 180°F (82°C) on an instant-read thermometer. Do not allow the mixture to boil.

Remove the pan from the heat and fish out the vanilla bean. Strain the custard through a fine-mesh strainer into a bowl set into an ice bath. Cool to room temperature, stirring constantly. Refrigerate for 3 hours or overnight and then freeze in an ice cream maker according to manufacturer's instructions.

Salted Caramel Frappe

We were a bit hesitant to include this drink because we didn't want to appear gimmicky. Salted caramel seems to be everywhere these days. But there's a reason. The flavor is addictive. The quality of the ice cream is key here because if it's too sweet, it will kill the drink. Hit it right and you're in for a treat. We are lucky in Boston because we have access to a few local, small-batch ice cream brands that excel in this particular flavor.

½ cup (120 ml) very cold milk

1½ cups (210 g) premium salted caramel ice cream, about 3 generous scoops (see Resources, page 138)

1 tablespoon (15 g) brown sugar simple syrup (recipe follows)

Sprinkle coarse sea salt

MAKE IT WICKED:
Add 1 ounce (28 ml) bourbon in the blender after the simple syrup

—

Yield: One 12-ounce (355 ml) frappe

Pour the milk into the container of a blender. Add the ice cream, followed by the syrup. With the blender on a low setting, purée for about 15 to 30 seconds until the mixture is thick and smooth. (If using a mixer, start on the slow speed and accelerate after a few seconds.) Pour into a tall glass and top with a sprinkle of sea salt.

Brown Sugar Simple Syrup

Brown sugar adds a little depth of flavor to this kitchen staple. It is perfect for our Salted Caramel Frappe, but we bet you can find lots of other uses for it as well.

½ cup (115 g) packed light brown sugar

½ cup (120 ml) water

—

Yield: ½ cup (160 g)

In a medium saucepan over medium heat, bring the sugar and water to a simmer, stirring. Simmer about 3 minutes until sugar dissolves and mixture thickens slightly. Remove from the heat and cool completely. Transfer to a container and store, covered, in the refrigerator.

Darkest Chocolate Frappe

We all have memories of drinking chocolate frappes as kids—even if some of us were as misinformed as to call them milkshakes. This version emphasizes chocolate's deliciously dark notes, so it may not appeal to children—even without the alcohol.

½ cup (120 ml) very cold milk

2 tablespoons (38 g) Devilish Chocolate Sauce (recipe follows)

4 generous scoops premium chocolate ice cream, the darker the better (about 1½ cups [210 g])

MAKE IT WICKED: Add 2 ounces (60 ml) Tuaca or Licor 43 after the chocolate sauce

—

Yield: One 16-ounce (475 ml) or two 8-ounce (235 ml) frappes

Pour the milk into the container of a blender. Add the sauce, followed by the ice cream. With the blender on a low setting, purée for about 15 to 30 seconds until the mixture is thick and smooth. (If using a mixer, start on the slow speed and accelerate after a few seconds.) Serve.

Devilish Chocolate Sauce

This sauce gets its dark color and complex flavor from black cocoa, which is a very rich, very dark Dutch-process cocoa powder (Dutching neutralizes the acidity). Black cocoa is used in Oreo cookies, so the sauce may cause childhood flashbacks.

1¾ cups (250 g) sugar

½ cup (43 g) unsweetened cocoa powder

½ cup (43 g) black cocoa (see Resources, page 138)

Pinch kosher salt

1 cup (235 ml) water

1 teaspoon (5 ml) vanilla

—

Yield: 1¾ cups (560 g)

In a medium saucepan, whisk the sugar, cocoa powders, and salt to combine. Over medium heat, whisk in the water. Continue whisking, breaking up the cocoa clumps, until the mixture boils. Boil for 3 minutes, stirring occasionally.

Remove from the heat and stir in the vanilla. Cool completely and transfer to a squeeze bottle. Store in the refrigerator for up to 2 weeks.

That's a Frappe!

Root Beer Float

One of us (don't ask) has been around long enough to remember when a certain root beer, recognizable by its orange and brown logo, was not a national supermarket staple. Rather, it was a special beverage available only at the company's own restaurants—usually roadside stands selling drinks, burgers, and ice cream, none of which had made it to the East Coast yet. It was at one of these stands, during a cross-country trip in the early 1970s, that one of us first experienced a root beer float. The root beer may not really have been that much better than any previously sampled. But sipping it on a dusty road in the heart of America, watching the sun set and a scoop of vanilla ice cream slip down the side of the frosty mug, it sure made an impression.

1 quart (1 L) root beer
 (your favorite brand)

4 generous scoops Vanilla
Ice Cream (page 128)

—

Yield: 4 servings

Pour the root beer into 4 tall glasses or frosty mugs, leaving some room at the top (the root beer will fizz after you add the ice cream). Place a scoop of ice cream in each glass, pressing it down on the rim of each glass. Serve with straws and long-handled spoons.

Ginger Beer Float

Making floats (and ice cream sodas) is something of a lost art. All too often, we find these soda fountain treats sloppily presented with the ice cream carelessly plopped into the beverage. Sure, that's where it eventually ends up, but the purists among us believe there is a process that should be observed, and it starts with the placement of the ice cream—resting on the side of the glass, rather than floating in the drink. In this twist on a soda fountain classic, the kick of the spicy ginger beer is a perfect foil to the silky, sweet coconut ice cream.

1 quart (1 L) ginger beer (your
favorite brand)

4 generous scoops Coconut Ice
Cream (recipe follows)

MAKE IT WICKED:
Turn your float into a Dark and
Stormy float by stirring 2
ounces (60 ml) of rum into
each glass of ginger beer
before adding the ice cream.

—

Yield: 4 floats

Pour the ginger beer into 4 tall glasses, leaving room at the top (the ginger beer will fizz after you add the ice cream). Place a scoop of ice cream on the rim of each glass, partially immersed in the ginger beer. Serve with straws and long-handled spoons.

Coconut Ice Cream

1½ cups (355 ml) whole milk

1½ cups (355 ml) heavy cream, divided

1 cup (85 g) dried, shredded, unsweetened coconut

Pinch of sea salt

5 egg yolks

¾ cup (150 g) sugar

SPECIAL EQUIPMENT:
Candy thermometer, ice cream maker

—

Yield: 1 quart (1 L)

In a heavy-bottomed saucepan over medium heat, combine the milk, 1 cup (235 ml) of the cream, coconut, and salt. Cook until you see small bubbles form around the edges of the pan. Remove from the heat, cover, and let steep for ½ hour. Strain through a fine-mesh strainer into a metal bowl and then return to pan.

In the bowl of an electric mixer fitted with the paddle attachment, beat the egg yolks and sugar on medium speed until they are light, about 2 to 3 minutes. Stir in the remaining ½ cup (120 ml) cream.

Reheat the coconut mixture for 2 minutes. Gradually beat ½ cup (60 ml) of warm coconut mixture into the egg mixture until smooth.

Pour the egg mixture into the coconut mixture remaining in the saucepan and cook, stirring constantly, over medium heat, until the mixture thickens enough to coat the back of a spoon and registers just barely 180°F (82°C). Scrape the bottom of the pan as you stir. Do not let the mixture boil or go over 180°F (82°C) or it will curdle.

Remove the pan from the heat. Pour the custard into a bowl and cool to room temperature. Cover and refrigerate for 3 to 24 hours.

Pour the custard into an ice cream maker and freeze according to the manufacturer's instructions.

Pistachio-Gelato Burger

This dessert burger was inspired by a fanatic's quest. Like starving desert wanderers chasing a mirage, Andrea and her husband once schlepped for several city blocks on a hot August afternoon in search of ice cream sandwiches—on brioche!—that they had heard were being dispensed through the window of some hole-in-the-wall near New York City's Union Square Greenmarket. It was worth every sweaty step. We have no idea if the place still exists, but it doesn't matter. We figured out how to make them at home.

12 Brioche Buns (recipe follows)

1 quart (1 L) Pistachio Gelato, slightly softened (recipe follows)

Devilish Chocolate Sauce (page 131)

—

Yield: 12 gelato burgers

Slice the buns in half horizontally. Place a large scoop of gelato on the bottom half of each bun. Spoon the chocolate sauce over the gelato and set the top halves of buns on top, pressing down lightly so the gelato spreads to the edges of the bun. Serve immediately.

GELATO VS. ICE CREAM

Gelato is the Italian name for ice cream. The word itself means frozen, and in Italy gelato can refer to any frozen dessert that is churned with milk or cream. Traditionally, gelato is more dense than American ice cream because gelato equipment is designed to incorporate less air into the mixture. It has less butterfat—often, more milk and less cream. And it tends to be less sweet, allowing the natural flavors to shine.

Brioche Buns

1 package (2½ teaspoons) active dry yeast

Pinch sugar, plus 2 tablespoons (26 g)

½ cup (120 ml) warm water

1½ cups (206 g) bread flour

1 cup (125 g) all-purpose flour, plus additional for sprinkling

¾ teaspoon (1 g) salt

1 stick (½ cup, 112 g) unsalted butter, room temperature, cut into 8 pieces

3 eggs, beaten

SPECIAL EQUIPMENT:
2 jelly-roll pans, parchment paper or silicone mats

—

Yield: 16 buns

In a small bowl, stir the yeast, pinch of sugar, and warm water until the yeast dissolves. Let stand about 10 minutes, until foamy.

In the bowl of a stand mixer fitted with the paddle attachment, combine the flours, remaining 2 tablespoons (26 g) sugar, and salt. Add the dissolved yeast, beating until combined. With the mixer on low, add the butter, 1 piece at a time, beating well after each addition. Beat in the eggs.

Change to a dough hook and knead for 4 to 5 minutes. The dough should start to pull away from the sides of the bowl. If it doesn't, add more flour, 1 tablespoon (8 g) at a time, until it does. It will still be somewhat sticky, but you should be able to transfer it from the bowl to the counter easily.

Sprinkle some flour on a clean counter and with lightly floured hands, knead the dough for about 5 minutes until it is smooth and elastic. Shape the dough into a ball and place it into a well-oiled bowl. Cover with a dish towel and let rise in a warm place until doubled in size, 1½ to 2 hours.

Line 2 jelly-roll pans with parchment paper or silicone mats.

Punch the dough down and knead several times. Using a metal pastry scraper, divide the dough into 16 even pieces. Roll each piece into a 1½-inch (3.5 cm) ball and place on the prepared jelly-roll pans. Cover with kitchen towels and let rise in a warm place until they are roughly doubled in size, another 1½ hours. (If you are making these buns for savory burgers and want them larger, separate into 8 or 12 larger pieces and roll into larger balls.)

Preheat the oven to 400°F (200°C, gas mark 6).

Bake the buns on the top and middle racks of the oven until golden brown, about 13 minutes, rotating about halfway through baking. (Baking time may vary slightly if the buns are larger.) Transfer to a rack and cool completely.

Pistachio Gelato

1 cup (123 g) shelled, unsalted pistachio nuts, divided

¾ cup (150 g) sugar, divided

2½ cups (570 ml) milk

½ cup (120 ml) heavy cream

1 teaspoon (5 ml) almond extract

5 egg yolks

SPECIAL EQUIPMENT: Ice cream maker

—

Yield: About 1 quart (1 L)

In the bowl of a food processor fitted with the chopping blade, finely grind ¾ cup (92 g) pistachio nuts with ¾ cup (50 g) sugar.

In a medium saucepan over medium heat, combine the milk, cream, almond extract, and ground pistachios. Cook until you see small bubbles form around the edges of the pan. Remove from the heat, cover, and let steep for 1 hour. Strain the pistachio mixture through a fine-mesh strainer into a metal bowl, pressing down on the nuts to extract as much flavor as possible. Discard the pistachios.

In a medium bowl, whisk the egg yolks with remaining ½ cup (100 g) sugar until light and lemon-colored.

Gradually whisk the pistachio mixture into the egg yolks and then pour it into the saucepan. Cook over medium heat, stirring constantly, until the mixture thickens and coats the back of the spoon and registers just barely 180°F (82°C). Do not let the mixture boil or go over 180°F (82°C) or it will curdle.

Remove the pan from the heat. Pour the custard into a bowl set in an ice bath and stir until it cools to room temperature. Cover the bowl and refrigerate for 3 to 24 hours.

Pour the custard into the canister of an ice cream maker and freeze according to manufacturer's instructions. While the ice cream is churning, chop the remaining ¾ cup (31 g) pistachios. Five minutes before churning is finished, pour in the chopped pistachios.

Transfer to a freezer container and freeze for at least 4 hours (2, if you are making the Burgers).

Resources

Equipment

Cast-Iron Skillets
www.lodgemfg.com

Stainless Steel Pans
www.all-clad.com

Stand Mixer Grinder Attachments
www.kitchenaid.com
www.amazon.com

Stand-Alone Meat Grinders
www.westonsupply.com
www.stxinternational.com
www.lemproducts.com

Kettle Grill
www.weber.com

Gas Grills
www.weber.com

Grill Basket
www.amazon.com

Charcoal Chimney
www.weber.com

Instant-Read Meat Thermometer
www.thermoworks.com

Infrared Thermometer
www.thermoworks.com

Probe Thermometer
www.polder.com
www.amazon.com

Home Deep Fryer
www.williams-sonoma.com
www.amazon.com
www.target.com
www.brevilleusa.com
www.shopdelonghi.com
www.gopresto.com

French Fry Cutter
www.amazon.com

Home Sous Vide Cooker
www.sousvidesupreme.com

Kitchen Scale
www.oxo.com
www.surlatable.com
www.amazon.com

Drink Mixers
www.hamiltonbeach.com
www.amazon.com

Hard-to-Find Ingredients

Black Cocoa
www.kingarthurflour.com

Caul Fat
store.heritagefoodsusa.com

Cimarron Doc's Bar-B-Q Seasoning
www.cimarrondoc.com

Harissa
www.igourmet.com
kalustyans.com

Kewpie Mayonnaise
www.amazon.com

Preserved Lemon
kalustyans.com

Maggi Seasoning
www.amazon.com

New Mexico Chile Ground
www.americanspice.com

Porcini Powder
www.purcellmountainfarms.com
www.thespicehouse.com
www.amazon.com

Portobello Powder
www.purcellmountainfarms.com
www.americanspice.com

Salted Caramel Ice Cream
https://jenis.com/products/salty-caramel

Worcestershire Powder
www.americanspice.com
www.amazon.com

About the Authors

Andy Husbands, the award-winning chef/owner of Tremont 647, in Boston, has been enticing patrons with his adventurous American cuisine at the South End neighborhood restaurant and bar for well over a decade. A James Beard "Best Chef" semi-finalist, Andy competed in the sixth season of Fox television network's Hell's Kitchen with Gordon Ramsay. When he's not in the kitchen or working with his favorite charities, Andy is on the BBQ trail with his award-winning team, iQUE.

Chris Hart, winner of the Jack Daniels Invitational World Championship in 2009, has dominated the competition BBQ circuit for the past ten years with his team, iQUE. The team was the first group of northerners in barbecue history to win a World Championship. Chris spends his days developing software, but his passion for cooking barbecue has him following the competition BBQ trail on weekends, pitting his talents against the best pitmasters in the U.S. In 2010, Chris cooked an elaborate barbecue tasting menu at the James Beard House in New York City. In 2011, he competed in Food Network's inaugural season of Best in Smoke.

Andrea Pyenson has been writing about food for more than a decade and enjoying it for a lot longer than that. Her writing about food and travel has appeared in various publications, including the *Boston Globe*, edible Boston, edible Cape Cod, msn.com, oneforthetable.com, *Washington Post*, and *Fine Cooking*.

Index

A

Aioli
    Red Wine-Basil Aioli, 95
    Rosemary Aioli, 119
    Sesame Aioli, 110
    Spiced Aioli, 113
    Tartar Aioli, 66
Almonds, in Mango Chile Slaw, 88
Arugula
    Jesse's Bison Burger, 94
    Salmon Burger, 80
Aussie Special Sauce
    Gold Coast Burger, 105
    recipe, 107
Avocado, in Glo's Bean Salad, 31

B

Bacon
    Dilled Salmon Roe, 32
    Duck Fat Fries, 120
    Gold Coast Burger, 105
    Homage to Island Creek Oysters
      Burger, 65
    Pig Candy, 35
    647's Breakfast Burger, 89
Baguettes, in Banh Mi Burger, 98–100
Banh Mi Burger, 98–100
Basic BBQ Rub
    Hill Country Brisket Burger, 55
    Pit Sauce, 56
    recipe, 56
Basil leaves
    Basil Pesto, 69
    Herb Salad, 113
    Jesse's Bison Burger, 94
    Red Wine-Basil Aioli, 95
Basil Pesto
    Belted Cow Bistro Veal Parmigiana
      Burger, 67–69
    recipe, 69
Beans
    Beet Burger, 83–84
    Glo's Bean Salad, 31
Beef chuck. *See also* Ground beef/
  ground chuck
    Bulgogi Burger, 108
    Our Perfect Burger, 20–22
    Pastrami Burger, 70
Beef, grinding, 11. *See also* Ground
  beef/ground chuck

Beer, in Brat Burger, 50
Beets
    Beet Burger, 83–84
    Gold Coast Burger, 105
Best.Mayo.Ever
    Harissa Mayo, 104
    recipe, 23
Bibb lettuce, in Homage to Island
  Creek Oysters Burger, 65
Bison Burger, 94
Black cocoa, in Devilish Chocolate
  Sauce, 131
Brat Burger, 50
Bread crumbs. *See also* Panko
    Our Perfect Turkey Burger, 29–30
    Pork Corton, 101
Brioche Buns
    Pistachio-Gelato Burger, 134
    recipe, 136
    Salmon Burger, 80
    The Schlow Burger, 75
Brisket Burger, Hill Brisket, 55
Brown rice, in Beet Burger, 83–84
Brown Sugar Simple Syrup
    recipe, 129
    Salted Caramel Frappe, 129
Bulgogi Burger, 108
Buns. *See* Burger buns
Burger blends, 11, 13
Burger buns. *See also* Flour Bakery
  Burger Buns; Katie's Burger Buns;
  Mindy's Pretzel Buns
    Bulgogi Burger, 108
    Diner-Style Steamed
      Cheeseburgers, 73–74
    Gold Coast Burger, 105
    Jesse's Bison Burger, 94
    Mole-Spiced Turkey Burger, 87
    Tortilla-Wrapped New Mexican
      Chile Burger, 58–61
Burgers
    cooking methods, 14–16
    history of, 10
    resting, 15
    shaping, 13
Burger toppings. *See also* Condiments;
  Sauces
    Caramelized Onions, 107
    Crispy Onions, 76
    Dilled Salmon Roe, 32
    Fried Oysters, 66

Garlic Confit Jam, 41
Grilled Romaine, 40
Jack D'Or Mustard, 43
Parsley Salad, 104
Peppered Onion Rings, 39
Pickled Green Tops, 36
Pig Candy, 35
Quick-Pickled Onions, 57
Spiced and Creamed Shimeji
  Mushrooms, 40
Tomato-Ginger Ketchup, 43
Triple Crème Stinky Cheese, 44

C

Cabbage
    Mango Chile Slaw, 88
    Quick Kimchi, 110
Caramelized Onions
    Gold Coast Burger, 105
    recipe, 107
Carrot, in Banh Mi Burger, 98–100
Cast iron skillets, 16
Charcoal grilling, 15–16
Cheese
    Basil Pesto, 69
    Belted Cow Bistro Veal Parmigiana
      Burger, 67–69
    Diner-Style Steamed
      Cheeseburgers, 73–74
    Gold Coast Burger, 105
    Jesse's Bison Burger, 94
    Josh Ozersky's Favorite Burger,
      62–63
    Lamb Juicy Lucy, 92
    Mindy's Pepper Jack Cheese Sauce,
      53
    Pastrami Burger, 71
    The Schlow Burger, 75
    Tortilla-Wrapped New Mexican
      Chile Burger, 58–61
    Triple Crème Stinky Cheese, 44
    Wicked Good Poutine, 122
Cheeseburgers, Diner-Style Steamed,
  73–74
Chickpea Burger, Moroccan, 103
Chives
    Green Krack Sauce, 123
    Salmon Burger, 80
    Wicked Good Poutine, 122
Chuck. *See* Beef chuck

141

Cilantro
    Green Krack Sauce, 123
    Herb Salad, 113
    Spiced Aioli, 113
    Tortilla-Wrapped New Mexican
       Chile Burger, 58–61
Cocoa powder, in Devilish Chocolate
  Sauce, 131
Coconut Ice Cream
    Ginger Beer Float, 132
    recipe, 133
Condiments. *See also* Aioli; Ketchup;
  Mayonnaise; Sauces
    Creamy Garlic Mustard, 44
    on Our Perfect Turkey Burger, 29
    Quick Kimchi, 110
    Russian Dressing, 71
Corn, in Glo's Bean Salad, 31
Cornmeal
    Fried Oysters, 66
    Peppered Onion Rings, 39
Corn tortilla, in Mole-Spiced Turkey
  Burger, 87
Creamy Garlic Mustard, 44
Creek Oysters, in Fried Oysters, 66
Creole Fries, 119
Crispy Onions
    recipe, 76
    The Schlow Burger, 75
Cucumber
    Banh Mi Burger, 98–100
    Glo's Bean Salad, 31
    Gram's Bread and Butter Pickles, 26
    Herb Salad, 113
    Lamb Juicy Lucy, 92
    Quick Kimchi, 110
    Tzatziki Sauce, 112

D

Darkest Chocolate Frappe, 131
Devilish Chocolate Sauce
    Darkest Chocolate Frappe, 131
    Pistachio-Gelato Burger, 134
    recipe, 131
Dilled Salmon Roe
    recipe, 32
    Salmon Burger, 80
Dill Mayonnaise
    recipe, 82
    Salmon Burger, 80
Diner-Style Steamed Cheeseburgers,
  73–74
Dinner rolls, in Josh Ozersky's Favorite
  Burger, 62–63
Doneness temperatures, 22
Dressings
    for Glo's Bean Salad, 31
    for Herb Salad, 113
    Russian Dressing, 71

Drink mixer, 17
Duck breasts, in Duck Fat Fries, 120

E

Egg rolls, in Moroccan Chickpea
  Burger, 103
Eggs
    Belted Cow Bistro Veal Parmigiana
      Burger, 67–69
    Brioche Buns, 136
    Gold Coast Burger, 105
    647's Breakfast Burger, 89
Egg yolks
    Best.Mayo.Ever., 23
    Coconut Ice Cream, 133
    Pistachio Gelato, 137
    Vanilla Ice Cream, 128
English muffins, in 647's Breakfast
  Burger, 89
Equipment, 16–17
Espelette pepper
    about, 38
    Peppered Onion Rings, 39
    Spiced and Creamed Shimeji
      Mushrooms, 40

F

Fast-food hamburger chain, first, 10
Fatback, in 647's Breakfast Sausage, 91
Fifth Dimension Powder
    Gold Coast Burger, 105
    Our Perfect Burger, 20–22
    recipe, 25
Fish, grinding, 11
Floats
    Ginger Beer Float, 132
    Root Beer Float, 132
Flour Bakery Burger Buns
    Beet Burger, 83–84
    Our Perfect Burger, 20
    recipe, 46–47
    The Schlow Burger, 75
Flour tortillas, in Tortilla-Wrapped
  New Mexican Chile Burger, 58–61
Frappes
    Salted Caramel Frappe, 129
    Vanilla Frappe, 126
Freezing grinder parts, 16
Freezing meat, 13
French fries. *See* Fries
Fried Oysters
    Homage to Island Creek Oysters
      Burger, 65
    recipe, 66
Fries
    Creole Fries, 119
    Duck Fat Fries, 120

    most common sizes for, 121
    Sweet Potato Pub Fries, 121
    Wicked Good Fries, 116–118

G

Garlic Butter
    Hill Country Brisket Burger, 55
    recipe, 57
Garlic Confit Jam, 41
Gas grills, 17
Gelato
    Pistachio Gelato, 137
    Pistachio-Gelato Burger, 134
Ginger Beer Float, 132
Ginger, fresh
    Banh Mi Burger, 98–100
    Bulgogi Burger, 108
    Quick Kimchi, 110
    Sesame Aioli, 110
    Tomato-Ginger Ketchup, 43
Glo's Bean Salad, 31
Gold Coast Burger, 105
Gram's Bread and Butter Pickles, 26
Greek yogurt
    Lamb Juicy Lucy, 92
    Tzatziki Sauce, 112
Green Chile Relish, in Tortilla-
  Wrapped New Mexican Chile Burger,
  58–61
Griddle, cooking burgers on a, 14–15
Grills and griddles, 16–17
Grinder parts, freezing, 13, 16
Grinders, 13, 16
Grinding meat, 11–13
Ground beef/ground chuck
    Bulgogi Burger, 108
    Diner-Style Steamed
      Cheeseburgers, 73–74
    Gold Coast Burger, 105
    Homage to Island Creek Oysters
      Burger, 65
    Josh Ozersky's Favorite Burger,
      62–63
    Our Perfect Burger, 20–22
    The Schlow Burger, 75
    Tortilla-Wrapped New Mexican
      Chile Burger, 58–61
Ground bison, in Jesse's Bison Burger,
  94
Ground lamb
    Gyro Burger, 111
    Lamb Juicy Lucy, 92
Ground pork
    Brat Burger, 50
    Homage to Island Creek Oysters
      Burger, 65
Ground turkey
    Mole-Spiced Turkey Burger, 87

142   **Quick and Easy Burger Cookbook**

Our Perfect Turkey Burger, 29–30
Ground veal
    Belted Cow Bistro Veal Parmigiana
      Burger, 67–69
    Brat Burger, 50
Gyro Burger, 111

H
Hamburger buns. *See* Burger buns
Harissa Mayo
    Moroccan Chickpea Burger, 103
    recipe, 104
Hill Country Brisket Burger, 55
Homage to Island Creek Oysters
  Burger, 65
Horseradish
    Russian Dressing, 71
    The Schlow Burger, 75

I
Iceberg lettuce, in Gold Coast Burger,
  105
Ice cream. *See also* Vanilla Ice Cream
    Coconut Ice Cream, 133
    Darkest Chocolate Frappe, 131
    gelato *vs.*, 134
    Ginger Beer Float, 132
    Salted Caramel Frappe, 129

J
Jack D'Or Mustard, 43
Jalapeño pepper
    Banh Mi Burger, 98–100
    Mango Chile Slaw, 88
Jesse's Bison Burger, 94
Josh Ozersky's Favorite Burger, 62–63

K
Kaiser rolls, in Belted Cow Bistro Veal
  Parmigiana Burger, 67–69
Katie's Burger Buns
    Homage to Island Creek Oysters
      Burger, 65
    Our Perfect Turkey Burger, 29
    recipe, 45
    Salmon Burger, 80
Ketchup
    Pit Sauce, 56
    Russian Dressing, 71
    Tomato-Ginger Ketchup, 43
Kettle grills, 16–17
Kewpie mayonnaise, in Aussie Special
  Sauce, 107

L
Lamb. *See* Ground lamb
Lettuce(s). *See also* Arugula
    Banh Mi Burger, 98–100

Beet Burger, 83–84
Gold Coast Burger, 105
Grilled Romaine, 40
Homage to Island Creek Oysters
  Burger, 65
Our Perfect Turkey Burger, 29–30
Live-fire cooking, 15–16

M
Mango Chile Slaw
    Mole-Spiced Turkey Burger, 87
    recipe, 88
Mayonnaise
    Aussie Special Sauce, 107
    Banh Mi Burger, 98–100
    Best.Mayo.Ever., 23
    Dill Mayonnaise, 82
    Harissa Mayo, 104
    Russian Dressing, 71
    The Schlow Burger, 75
Meat, grinding, 11–13
Milkshakes. *See* Frappes
Mindy's Pepper Jack Cheese Sauce
    Brat Burger, 50
    recipe, 53
Mindy's Pretzel Buns
    Brat Burger, 50
    recipe, 52
Mint, fresh
    Beet Burger, 83–84
    Glo's Bean Salad, 31
    Gyro Burger, 111
    Herb Salad, 113
    Lamb Juicy Lucy, 92
    Tzatziki Sauce, 112
Mole-Spiced Turkey Burger, 87
Moroccan Chickpea Burger, 103
Mushrooms
    Beet Burger, 83
    Spiced and Creamed Shimeji
      Mushrooms, 40
Mustards
    Creamy Garlic Mustard, 44
    Jack D'Or Mustard, 43

N
New Mexican green chiles, Tortilla-
  Wrapped New Mexican Chile Burger,
  58–61
Nuts
    Basil Pesto, 69
    Mango Chile Slaw, 88
    Pistachio Gelato, 137

O
Onions. *See also* Red onion; Yellow
  onions
    Caramelized Onions, 107

Crispy Onions, 76
Peppered Onion Rings, 39
Quick-Pickled Onions, 57
Our Perfect Burger, 20–22
Our Perfect Turkey Burger, 29–30
Oysters, Fried, 66

P
Pale ale, in Mindy's Pretzel Buns, 52
Panko
    Banh Mi Burger, 98–100
    Beet Burger, 83–84
    Belted Cow Bistro Veal Parmigiana
      Burger, 67–69
    Salmon Burger, 80
Parsley, fresh
    Duck Fat Fries, 120
    Garlic Butter, 57
    Jesse's Bison Burger, 94
    Lamb Juicy Lucy, 92
    Moroccan Chickpea Burger, 103
    Our Perfect Turkey Burger, 29–30
    Parsley Salad, 104
    Salmon Burger, 80
Parsley Salad
    Moroccan Chickpea Burger, 103
    recipe, 104
Pastrami, in Pastrami Burger, 70
Peanuts, Mango Chile Slaw, 88
Peppered Onion Rings, 39
Peppers. *See also* Espelette pepper
    Glo's Bean Salad, 31
    Gram's Bread and Butter Pickles, 26
    Mole-Spiced Turkey Burger, 87
    roasting, 87
Pickled beets, in Gold Coast Burger,
  105
Pickled Green Tops, 36
Pickles
    Gram's Bread and Butter Pickles,
      26
    Tartar Aioli, 66
Pig Candy, 35
Pineapple, in Gold Coast Burger, 105
Pine nuts, in Basil Pesto, 69
Pistachio Gelato
    Pistachio-Gelato Burger, 134
    recipe, 137
Pita bread
    Gyro Burger, 111
    Lamb Juicy Lucy, 92
Pit Sauce
    Hill Country Brisket Burger, 53
    recipe, 56
Porcini powder, in Fifth-Dimension
  Powder, 25
Pork Corton
    Banh Mi Burger, 98–100
    recipe, 101

Index 143

Pork, ground. *See* Ground pork
Pork shoulder/butt
    Banh Mi Burger, 98–100
    Pork Corton, 101
    647's Breakfast Sausage, 91
Portobello mushroom, in Beet Burger, 83–84
Portobello powder, in Fifth-Dimension Powder, 25
Potatoes. *See* Wicked Good Fries
Poultry, grinding, 11
Poutine, Wicked Good, 122

Q

Quick Kimchi
    Bulgogi Burger, 108
    recipe, 110
Quick-Pickled Onions
    Hill Country Brisket Burger, 55
    recipe, 57

R

Ramps, in Pickled Green Tops, 36
Red Wine-Basil Aioli
    Jesse's Bison Burger, 94
    recipe, 95
Resting burgers, 15
Romaine, Grilled, 40
Root Beer Float, 132
Rosemary Aioli, 119
Russian Dressing
    Pastrami Burger, 71
    recipe, 71
Rye bread, in Pastrami Burger, 71

S

Sage leaves, fresh
    Homage to Island Creek Oysters Burger, 65
    647's Breakfast Sausage, 91
Salads
    Herb Salad, 113
    Parsley Salad, 104
Salmon Burger, 80
Salmon roe, in Dilled Salmon Roe, 32
Salted Caramel Frappe, 129
Sandwich bread/buns
    Belted Cow Bistro Veal Parmigiana Burger, 67–69
    Hill Country Brisket Burger, 55
Sauces. *See also* Aioli
    Aussie Special Sauce, 107
    for Bulgogi Burger, 108
    Green Krack Sauce, 123
    Mindy's Pepper Jack Cheese Sauce, 53
    Pit Sauce, 56
    for The Schlow Burger, 75

Tomato Sauce, 69
    Tzatziki Sauce, 112
Sauerkraut, in Pastrami Burger, 70
The Schlow Burger, 75
Sesame Aioli
    Bulgogi Burger, 108
    recipe, 110
Shallots
    Beet Burger, 83
    Dilled Salmon Roe, 32
    Dill Mayonnaise, 82
    Spiced Aioli, 113
    Spiced and Creamed Shimeji Mushrooms, 40
Shimeji Mushrooms, Spiced and Creamed, 40
Side dishes. *See also* Salads
    Glo's Bean Salad, 31
    Mango Chile Slaw, 88
    Mole-Spiced Turkey Burger, 87
647's Breakfast Burger, 89
647's Breakfast Sausage
    647's Breakfast Burger, 89
    recipe, 91
Skillets, 14–15, 16
Smoking, basics of, 42
Sour cream
    Creamy Garlic Mustard, 44
    Russian Dressing, 71
    Spiced and Creamed Shimeji Mushrooms, 40
Sous vide cooker, 17
Spiced Aioli, 113
Standalone meat grinder, 13, 16
Sweet Potato Dust, 121
Sweet Potato Pub Fries, 121

T

Tartar Aioli
    Homage to Island Creek Oysters Burger, 65
    recipe, 66
Temperatures, doneness, 22
Thermometers, 17
Thyme, fresh
    Beet Burger, 83
    Duck Fat Fries, 120
    Garlic Confit Jam, 41
Togarashi pepper
    about, 38
    Peppered Onion Rings, 39
Tomatoes
    Gold Coast Burger, 105
    Gyro Burger, 111
    Jesse's Bison Burger, 94
    Tomato-Ginger Ketchup, 43
    Tomato Sauce, 69

Tomato-Ginger Ketchup
    Beet Burger, 83–84
    recipe, 43
Tomato Sauce
    Belted Cow Bistro Veal Parmigiana Burger, 67–69
    recipe, 69
Tortilla-Wrapped New Mexican Chile Burger, 58–61
Triple Crème Stinky Cheese, 44
Turkey. *See* Ground turkey
Tzatziki Sauce
    Gyro Burger, 111
    recipe, 112

V

Vanilla bean
    Vanilla Frappe, 126
    Vanilla Ice Cream, 128
Vanilla Frappe, 126
Vanilla Ice Cream
    recipe, 128
    Root Beer Float, 132
    Vanilla Frappe, 126
Vinaigrette, Duck Fat, 120

W

Wicked Good Fries
    Creole Fries with, 119
    Duck Fat Fries, 120
    Gyro Burger, 111
    recipe, 116–118
    Wicked Good Poutine, 122
Wicked Good Poutine, 122
Wood-fired cooking, 15–16

Y

Yuzu juice, in Green Krack Sauce, 123

Z

Zucchini, in Beet Burger, 83–84